The problems of theology

The problems of theology

BRIAN HEBBLETHWAITE

Fellow and Dean of Chapel,
Queens' College, Cambridge
University Lecturer in Divinity

CAMBRIDGE UNIVERSITY PRESS

Cambridge
London   New York   New Rochelle
Melbourne   Sydney

Published by the Press Syndicate of the University of Cambridge
The Pitt Building, Trumpington Street, Cambridge CB2 1RP
32 East 57th Street, New York, NY 10022, USA
296 Beaconsfield Parade, Middle Park, Melbourne 3206, Australia

First published 1980

Photoset, printed and bound in Great Britain by
REDWOOD BURN LIMITED
Trowbridge & Esher

British Library Cataloguing in Publication Data

Hebblethwaite, Brian Leslie
  The problems of theology.
  1. Theology
  I. Title
  201'.1   BR118   79–41812

  ISBN 0 521 23104 3 hard covers
  ISBN 0 521 29811 3 paperback

Contents

Preface

One of the main problems to be discussed in this book is the relation between theology and religious studies. There is a tendency these days towards treating every aspect of religion, including the theologies of the different religions, under the single, all-embracing heading of 'religious studies'. This creates a fundamental problem for theologians in any particular religious tradition; for, as I argue in Chapter 1, the primary meaning of the term 'theology', controlling its looser and wider senses, is rational talk about God. The 'believing theologian', as I call him, is bound to resist the reduction of his activities to one among many interesting phenomena in the many-sided world of religion, to be studied as a more or less valuable historical curiosity. 'Theology', as I say, has a primary sense and a number of looser and wider senses. It can be used simply to refer to the different disciplines to be found within a traditional theological faculty. I argue that such disciplines must be related to theology in its primary meaning, if their presence in a single 'theological' faculty is to be defended. But I do not suggest that theology is for believers only. I discuss the question, in what sense it is possible for atheists to be theologians, and suggest a way of thinking of theology as consisting of serious, open questions, well worth studying for their own sake in the university, with all the critical and scholarly tools available there. Theology, then, is neither a closed, in-group activity for believers, nor just an intriguing aspect of the history of religions. Further problems explored in this book include the relations between theology and the comparative study of religions, be-

Preface

tween theology and the social sciences, between theology and philosophy, and between theology and history. I try to take seriously the alleged claims to revelation which the religions have made, and to answer the question whether, in the face of cultural and historical relativism, doctrinal theology can still be carried on today. In addition, there is a chapter on the problems of theology and ethics (both individual and social). In the nature of the case, the discussion of so many different problems in such a short book is brief and introductory. But, as well as introducing the reader to a rich and varied field of study, I aim to suggest a particular hypothesis about the proper nature and scope of theology today.

Is there such a subject?

Introduction

In most of the universities of western Europe, there survives a faculty of Christian theology (occasionally more
than one, as in the Protestant and Catholic faculties at
some German universities). In colleges of education, in
some newer universities, and, increasingly, in schools, if
the subject is studied at all, it is more likely to be under
the heading of 'religious studies'. Nevertheless there are
departments of theology, there are such people as theologians, and a surprisingly large number of theological
books are still being published. Even in religious studies,
theology appears as one among many phenomena in the
whole world of religion.

To ask, then, Is there such a subject?, might seem to be
a foolish question. For clearly there is. Is it not more sensible to ask, What is theology?, What do theologians
think they are doing?, Ought there still to be theology
faculties in the universities? But I stick by the question in
this chapter's title for the following reason. The word
'theology' means rational thought or talk about God,
and this is what, for the most part, theologians have held
their subject to be. But we live in a time when the majority of educated people in the west do not believe in God.
For them there is, strictly speaking, no such subject as
theology; for its subject matter or object does not exist.
Of course it is easy to reply that the beliefs existed once
and still, to some extent at least, do exist. We can study
the scriptures and other writings in which men's beliefs
in God have found expression, and we can study the

history of religious belief in God, just as we can study any other aspect of religion. Isn't that what theology really is – the study of *belief* in God?

By going along with this view it might appear that we *can* subsume theology under the wider and more secure umbrella of religious studies. Two further points tend to reinforce this view. Firstly not all religions include or imply theology. We have, in religious studies, to reckon with the non-theistic religions such as Theravada Buddhism and certain strands in Hinduism, and also with religions such as Jainism, Taoism and Confucianism, which treat belief in God or the gods as relatively unimportant. Secondly we have to reckon with the plurality of theistic religions, each involving its own theology. We can study Hindu theology, Jewish theology, Christian theology, Muslim theology and so on. On these grounds, too, we might suppose that theology is best thought of as a relatively restricted (though pluriform) branch of religious studies.

If we accept these lines of argument, we are still left with the problem expressed in the title of this chapter. We may have rescued theology from uncertainty about its alleged object, but we have not thereby succeeded in defending the singling out of Christian theology as an academic subject in western universities. For if Christian theology is but one aspect of one theistic stream within the wider history of religions, how can we defend restriction of academic interest to it alone? No doubt something can be said about the impossibility of studying the whole sphere of religion and about the importance of Christianity in the history of the west, but there remains a suspicion of arbitrariness, especially in the university financed by the state, if we insist on the study of Christian theology alone.

On the other hand no theologian, in any theistic tradition, will accept the reduction of his discipline to one aspect of religious studies. The reason for this can perhaps be brought out if we put the matter hypothetically. If God exists, the theologian will argue, then theology is concerned not just with the different beliefs of the theistic religions within the wider religious life of man, but rather with the realities of God, man and the universe in their true nature and interrelation. In other words, if God exists, it is not religious studies which includes theology, but theology which includes religious studies along with everything else.

Here is a problem indeed. It is by far the greatest of the problems with which this book is concerned. On the one hand theology, as understood by its practitioners, seems to depend on a widely disputed premise, namely, the existence of God. On the other hand *if* God exists, then theology has good reason to claim to be dealing with the ultimate reality behind all other realities, all other objects of study which there may be.

On any view, however, theology itself must reckon with the plurality of theistic and non-theistic religions in the world. Even if God does exist and can be thought about rationally in the discipline known as theology, each religious tradition which claims to provide knowledge of God must have something to say about the different claims of the other religions. Each tradition's theology, therefore, must include from its own standpoint the theology *of* religion and the religions, the attempt, that is, to *explain* the plurality of religions. We shall try to keep this in mind throughout the book as a problem affecting all the other problems which we explore.

One further question arises from what has just been said. Can an atheist be a theologian? Clearly an atheist can study religion; but if theology is concerned with the reality of God, then surely it presupposes belief? It must be done from the inside by those who actually believe in God. Otherwise one is just studying other people's belief, and theology once again is swallowed up as an aspect of religious studies. The question is not, however, quite so easily answered as that. You will recall that the notion of theology as the wider discipline, as concerned with God, man and the universe in their true nature and interrelation, was introduced hypothetically. If God exists, that is the proper status of theology. Now an atheist can entertain hypotheses. If he is prepared to enter sympathetically into the *possibility* that God exists, he will be able to appreciate what theologians working from within the world of belief are doing, and, indeed, perhaps contribute to their work. For the believing theologian in the modern world must keep in mind the fact that God's existence is disputed, and must be prepared to scrutinise the arguments and grounds for and against belief in God. The interchange between believer and unbeliever over the grounds for belief as well as over the rationality of what is said from within belief is important for theology. Theologians cannot live in a private world, least of all in the university.

More will be said about this problem of the degree to which theology presupposes belief when we come to consider the methods of theology. But it needs to be pointed out at once that this compromise solution to the question, Can an atheist be a theologian?, whereby the interchange between believer and unbeliever is seen to be helpful to the theological enterprise, is possible only on two conditions, one on the believer's side and one on the unbeliever's side.

On the believer's side this solution will work only if theology is recognised to be a thoroughly self-critical and rational discipline, and if believing theologians are prepared to enter into open-minded discussion with unbelieving ones and with their colleagues in other fields. We shall see that there are ways of understanding theology which on religious grounds rule out such self-criticism of the bases of theology. If they are right, theology's place in the university is highly dubious. It would be much more reasonable to restrict it to seminaries and schools of divinity set up by churches themselves.

On the unbeliever's side this solution will work only if the notion of God's existence is admitted as both important and not obviously false. The scholar who *presupposes* that all religion is wish-fulfilment or a solace in unjust social conditions will be quite unable to make any contribution to theology or to see the point of there being such a subject, let alone its place in the university.

If theology remains open and self-critical, and if the fundamental questions of truth and meaning with which it deals are acknowledged to be both important and unsettled, then there is a strong case for keeping theology as an independent discipline and refusing to let it be swallowed up by religious studies.

Of all academic subjects, however, theology is the most precarious. Yet in claiming to deal with fundamental questions of truth and meaning it sets a salutary question mark against the assumptions of more manageable disciplines. We have insisted that neither believer nor unbeliever is absolved from some anxiety where theology is concerned. Both will be tempted to take refuge in the more secure sphere of the scientific study and the comparative study of religion. But both may find themselves admitting that truth will be served less well if they do so. The university (and the state), one hopes, will maintain faculties of theology, if they see in them the search for ultimate truth rigorously and responsibly pursued.

Theology may be a particularly precarious subject, but it is not unique in carrying such anxieties. The human sciences, generally, provoke existential questions. Sociology frequently puts the way of life of its own practitioners in question. History constantly confronts the student with warnings to himself and his society. No one can study English without being forced by great literature to ask about the meaning of his own life and that of his society. Even the natural sciences, paradigms of objectivity and rigorous method, confront the scholar with agonising moral choices: Is research into the genetic material to carry on regardless of the consequences for the future of man? A discipline which investigates the question whether or not these and other problems are to be faced in the context of an ultimate horizon of meaning is not to be despised. Certainly those states (and universities) which have abolished faculties of theology appear to have solved neither the theoretical nor the practical problems of understanding and living in the world.

The object of theology

It was pointed out at the beginning that the word 'theology' means rational thought or talk about God. If we are to accept this definition, we need to meet a number of powerful objections, both from the side of philosophy and from that of theology itself.

Theologians cannot even begin their work unless they have some preliminary notion of what the word 'God' might mean. We have to remember that an influential group of philosophers profess themselves unable to attach any meaning to the word at all. However, this is little more than a sceptical gambit, and there is no reason why one cannot begin with certain extremely simple, even naive, definitions such as anyone might be inclined to give. 'Creator of the world' is one such definition; another is 'the mind or will or spirit behind the universe'; a third might be something like 'ultimate reality conceived of as personal, worshipful, giving meaning to the world and to life'. All kinds of objections spring to mind on being offered such definitions, but to criticise them and refine them is to begin to do theology.

Certain basic questions, however, are obviously being begged in the attempt to specify the concept of God by means of such provisional definitions. They reflect the understanding of God as personal creator fostered in religions such as Judaism, Christianity and Islam. It is possible to begin at a less question-begging, more philosophical, if vaguer level by speaking, as the German theologian Wolfhart Pannenberg does, of God as 'the all-determining reality'. Towards the end of the previous section, I myself attempted to locate the area of theological concern even more vaguely by speaking of 'an ultimate horizon of meaning'. Similarly the German–American theologian, Paul Tillich, used vague phrases such as 'ultimate reality' and 'ground of being' in the attempt to locate talk of God.

It is important, at some stage, to try to press back from the more specific notions fostered in particular theistic traditions to more philosophical and more general notions, which do not presuppose alleged self-revelations of a personal creator. This is necessary if there is to be dialogue between, say, the Hindu theologian and the Christian theologian, let alone between believer and unbeliever. But it is far from clear that we have to begin so far back. On the other hand it would obviously be a mistake to begin with highly specific developed notions of God such as 'the Blessed Trinity revealed in the incarnation of the Son of God in Jesus Christ'. For the word 'God' is not the private property of Christians and we must retain some links with its more general use in the history of religions and in different religious traditions today. The rough definitions which I suggested as a starting point, such as 'creator of the world', involve some selectivity from the many different ideas of God or the gods to be found in the history of religions, but it is not an arbitrary selection, given the actual course of the development of the great monotheistic faiths in world history.

Adopting some such rough and ready starting point as a provisional indication of what the theologian is talking about, we recognise straight away that it is a mistake to think of the word 'God' as a name. The logician Peter Geach has pointed out that 'God' functions as a descriptive term.* It is more like 'the prime minister' than 'Mrs Thatcher'.

The object of theology, then, can be thought of as the ultimate reality whom certain religions teach us to think of as personal creator and lord of the universe (though we realise that it is disputed even within the world of religion whether we can assume that ultimate reality is personal).

From the side of theology itself comes quite a different objection to the notion that we can speak of God as the object of theology. Protestant Christianity, especially in Germany, has fought shy of the implication that the human mind can treat God as an object, least of all as an object of rational enquiry. God must be thought of, according to this school, always as subject. His reality is invariably misconceived when we think we have him within the grasp of human knowledge. This is a serious objection, and needs to be examined, not only by the *Christian* theologian. The dangers of what the Germans call 'objectification' in speaking of God are real, and will have to be borne in mind when we turn to the methods of theology. Suffice it to say here that a recognition of this problem need not deter us from the attempt to think and argue rationally, clearly (and reverently), about the one in whom we or our friends believe. This is quite compatible with admitting that God, if he exists, is not one object among others on the same level of existence as the things and persons in the world. Certainly, as we shall see, the unique nature of the object of theology determines our means of access to it. It would be irrational to think otherwise. But that does not mean that

* *God and the Soul* (London: Routledge and Kegan Paul, 1969), p. 108.

we should follow Paul Tillich in refusing to say either that God exists or that he does not exist. It is just confusing thus to restrict the term 'exists' to objects in the world, even if Tillich was trying thereby to make an important point about the ultimacy of God.

I have suggested that theology, in the sense of rational thought or talk about God, may be undertaken self-critically by the believing theologian and hypothetically be the atheist or agnostic. In what follows I attempt to describe the theological enterprise more precisely, with the example of the believing theologian chiefly in mind. My description, as will be obvious, is that of a believing theologian; but at the same time it is offered as an extended hypothesis, to be considered seriously by the unbeliever too.

How, then, might the would-be theologian proceed, given the rough and provisional characterisation of the object of his study, suggested in the preceding paragraphs? The next step would be to examine some examples of theological writing from the past and present of one or more of the great theistic faiths. The theologian, we learn, sets himself to achieve increasing sensitivity to the different ways in which men and women at different periods of history and in different cultural situations have expressed belief in God. Great stress has recently been laid in Christian theology upon the fact that the theologian must become aware of the degree to which conceptions of the nature of God, of the relation between God and the world, and of the way God works in the world, are conditioned by limited and changing categories of thought. But it is easy to exaggerate this point. The fact that the twentieth-century theologian has to explore what it means to speak of God in terms of his own cultural self-consciousness and in the light of modern knowledge of the world need not be held to cut him off from the faith and the theology of first-century or medieval men and women. To put the matter hypothetically once again, if God exists, ultimate reality remains the same despite man's changing understanding. It is perfectly true, however, that human categories of thought and understanding do change, and theological reflection has to take account of the changes.

The Christian theologian, like any other, has to become aware of the strangeness of, for example, first-century and medieval thought. Yet the superficial scanner of cultural change can easily be over-impressed by this awareness. To read the ancient and medieval theologians from Paul onwards is sometimes to move in a quite alien and incomprehensible world, but sometimes to catch glimpses of acute and permanent penetration into what it means to speak of God, and to see oneself and the world as related to God. Part of the Christian theologian's task is to trace the continuity in experience and understanding of God between Paul, Augustine, Luther, Calvin, Kierkegaard and Barth, to mention but one (branching) strand in the Christian tradition. Another example of what I call permanent penetration into the rationality of belief in God is to be found in Anselm's definition of God as 'that than which nothing greater can be conceived', another in Aquinas's grasp of the way in which human concepts must be applied analogically in making judgements about God. There is in Aquinas, the thirteenth-century systematic theologian (and saint), a most subtle awareness of the impossibility of treating God as one entity among others, as well as of the difficulties involved in projecting our language beyond its normal field of reference. To become a Christian theologian one would need to master the technical language of such men as Athanasius, Augustine, Anselm and Aquinas, not in order to juggle with the concepts like counters in a game, but in order to appreciate the genuine, if partial, perception of reality which they express, or at least to see the point of such claimed perception. The skill with which such men explored the implications of their theism is likely to win respect and admiration, as well as to illustrate concretely what it means to speak and think rationally about God. There is something enormously exciting about coming across a really great theological thinker, who, one realises, has grasped the possibility of articulating human consciousness of God in a comprehensive and communicable way. There is a transcending of the intellectual and cultural background in such figures that we must look for in our own world, but are unlikely to find if we have not recognised it in theirs.

It is also true that the reader of such authors will be struck by their limitations, by the peculiarities, for example, of the demonology and the apocalyptic views of the end of the present world order which Paul (and Jesus, probably) shared with contemporary Judaism. One may well be struck by the moral deficiencies of Anselm's theory of the atonement, or by the theoretical constrictions imposed on Aquinas's concept of the relation between God and the world by the philosophical notion of divine impassibility. Present day Christian theologians, moreover, are bound to suspect the over-confidence of the old confessions, whether on long agreed definitions or on matters which have come to demarcate denominational divisions.

The fact is that no formulation, past or present, of belief in God is going to satisfy entirely. If God exists, the living relation between God and man must be recognised to transcend men's intellectual capacities and to demand constant reformulation and new exploration both by individuals and by groups. It has already been stressed that any individual theologian's perception is conditioned to a greater or lesser extent by patterns of thought characteristic of his age. The theologian has to learn to detect the pervasiveness of such influences in his own time as in the past. But he must also learn to judge them, to see where irreversible development has taken place, and where certain aspects of a by-gone view are irretrievable. Nowhere is this more important than in respect of the changes in men's understanding of the world that have occurred since the seventeenth century and the rise of modern science. The bearing of the Enlightenment and of post-Enlightenment thought on theology and particularly on the way in which the relation between God and the world is represented is one of the most important problems for the modern theologian. From it derives the significance of the greatest individuals in nineteenth- and twentieth-century Christian theology, Friedrich Schleiermacher and Karl Barth. The two men responded to the situation in very different, indeed diametrically opposite ways; but they both were intensely aware of the necessity of taking account of post-Enlightenment thought – in Barth's case, very critical account – in articulating Christian theology today.

The point I am making can be put like this: it is no good simply for the Christian theologian to extract a selection of insights into talk about God from the great theologians past and present and to attempt to co-ordinate them systematically. Such insights have to be seen in relation to the overall problem of talk about God and the world created by the modern scientific world-view. Whatever we learn from Paul and Athanasius, Anselm and Aquinas, we cannot live in their world. Ours is the post-Enlightenment world, however fragmented and pluriform we find that world to be, and however critical about that world we may become. There have been changes of permanent significance since ancient and medieval times. Of course there are continuities as well. Just to cite one example: Aquinas's distinction between primary and secondary causality can still help the modern theologian to relate the language of theology and the language of science, and to articulate a viable conception of God's action in the world.*

* On this, see, further, p. 118, below.

Is there such a subject?

These are no more than hints to illustrate the problems of talk about God in modern theology. I have stressed both the continuities and the discontinuities between past ages and our own. The Christian theologian today can neither break with the past completely nor embrace the past uncritically. A few years ago, the so-called 'death of God' theologians made the first error, breaking with the past completely, accepting the 'end of theism' and looking for an entirely new 'this-worldly' understanding of Christianity. That path has been found to lead to a dead end. Now it is one thing to reject all talk of God or of a relation between God and the creation. But it is quite another to rethink, in the light of modern knowledge, the old ways of distinguishing the earthly and the heavenly, the natural and the supernatural. This task of reinterpretation is essential for the modern theologian; and indeed the really interesting questions posed by the Enlightenment concern the manner in which we are to conceive of the relation between God and the world and of the way God acts in the world.

It may be that such questions are misconceived and illusory; but such a conclusion should come at the end of the enquiry and not at the beginning. But the possibility that such questions are illusory underlines the need for the Christian theologian at some stage in his enterprise to re-examine the case for theism against atheism, and the case for personal theism against the impersonal monism of some at least of his Hindu colleagues. We shall return to these points in Chapter 4.

The methods of theology

The problem of theological method is particularly acute, since even if God does exist, he is clearly not accessible to us in the ways in which material objects, living creatures

13

The problems of theology

and human beings are. It is this consideration that gives plausibility to the view, mentioned earlier, that God, being Spirit, is accessible only to faith, and that only out of a living relationship to God can the truths of God be known and thought about. A neutral uncommitted approach, on this view, is simply inappropriate to the reality with which theology is concerned. A detached approach, it is argued, is appropriate in science, where by and large the relation between the observer and the world is external. The world is not affected by being observed (except at the level of sub-atomic particles). Experiments must be independent of personal involvement and repeatable irrespective of time and place. Such an approach, however, is only partially appropriate to our knowledge of human beings. Certainly one observes another person's body and his behaviour. The latter, including his linguistic, social and institutional behaviour, can be made the object of scientific study by psychologists and sociologists. But personal knowledge goes beyond these approaches. Here a difference in the nature of the objects to be known requires a different approach. The essence of personal knowledge, it is claimed, is given 'existentially' in and through personal relation. Of course our personal knowledge is greatly extended, through literature, biography and historical writing. We are not confined to knowledge by personal acquaintance. But unless we knew what persons and personal relationships are like from within, we should not be able to achieve these further imaginative extensions of personal knowledge. Our knowledge of God, the argument continues, is comparable only with this second aspect of personal knowledge. In no sense can we observe God; he can be known only from within the relationship of faith. For that is the only way in which God gives himself to be known.

It is difficult to quarrel with the general principle behind this argument, namely, that our access to any reality must be determined by and appropriate to the nature of the reality in question. This principle has been strongly defended by the Swiss theologian Karl Barth as essential to theological method. At one point in his *Church Dogmatics* he says that a man is no theologian and never will be one who does not make the following statement of Hilary of Poitiers his own as an axiom of method: *intelligentia dictorum ex causis est assumenda dicendi, quia non sermoni res, sed rei sermo subjectus est.** It is a little difficult to capture this in English without paraphrase, but freely translated it might run: 'the meaning of what we say must be gathered from what impels us to speak; for our talk is determined by its object, not vice versa'. Both the fourth-century Bishop of Poitiers and the leading theologian of the twentieth century had a firm grasp of what philosophers call a realist epistemology – that is, the view that it is how things actually are that determines our knowledge of them and what we say about them. No matter what we are talking about it is the reality itself which must be allowed to control our response, and what we say must be judged by the accuracy with which it corresponds with the reality in question.

Barth insists that this is an indispensable aspect of theological method. The theologian must let his talk of God be criticised and refined so that it corresponds better and better with the actuality of God. Here at least theology and science are comparable; for physics too requires an appropriate objectivity. The language of physics must be determined by the actual nature of the physical world and not by our own suppositions, however important a role these may play in the process of scientific discovery.

As I say, it is difficult to quarrel with this general

---

* Karl Barth, *Church Dogmatics*, I. 1, English trans. (Edinburgh: T. & T. Clark, 1936), p. 407.

principle or with Barth's insistence that it applies to theology. But the problem of access to the reality in question remains. Is it really true that God's reality is accessible only to faith? And even if it is, is faith so different from anything else that it cannot be discussed and probed by believer and unbeliever in dialogue? There is nothing irrational about the special case of God requiring a special mode of access; on the contrary it would be irrational to try to use inappropriate means (such as a camera or a tape-recorder) to obtain knowledge of God. But if faith is such a private and undiscussable mode of approach as Barth and others seem to suppose, then it is not surprising that this blocking off of the allegedly sole appropriate means of access to the living God from all debate and scrutiny has been accused of irrationality.

It has not always been thought in Christian theology that access to God is so restricted to the unique and undiscussable mode of faith. In earlier ages, rational arguments for the existence of God were advanced, and well-established authorities (Bible and church teaching) were appealed to for knowledge of God's revelation of himself to men. It would still, of course, require faith to enter into a personal relationship with God, but the reality of God and something of his nature were topics publicly discussable by agreed criteria. What has undermined this stance and driven theologians to take refuge in a *purely* private and internal mode of access to God is precisely the discovery since the time of the Enlightenment (a) of the shakiness of the alleged proofs of God's existence, (b) of the very human nature of the alleged sources of divine revelation – scripture and church teaching, and (c) of the comparable and conflicting claims made in other major religions of the world. All these matters have now become the objects of searching critical study, and the temptation has been to retreat to an unassailable private, inner basis for religion and theology alike.

Bishop J. A. T. Robinson has made us familiar with the distinction between 'beginning from above' and 'beginning from below', and has put in a powerful plea for beginning from below, from experience, from where people actually are, if we are to get anywhere both in religion and theology. Now it might appear that Barth's insistence on an appropriate objectivity and on letting our thoughts be controlled by the reality and self-revelation of God is a clear example of beginning from above. But curiously the difference between Barth and Robinson is not so great as might at first appear. Our discussion of the problem of access to the reality of God will have shown that neither Barth's faith-claims nor Robinson's experience-claims can guarantee the reality of their alleged object or the appropriateness of what is said about it. Certainly all theology begins from below in that it begins with things human beings, especially those with creative religious vision, actually say about God. We have agreed that the reality of God is not given to us directly in an unmediated way out of the blue. But if there is no guaranteed, sacrosanct, direct form of divine communication, then theology must subject all the alleged indirect channels of divine–human encounter – arguments, historical events, scriptures, traditions, faith-claims and experience-claims – to rigorous scrutiny and discussion. Thus it ought to be possible both to begin from below and to recognise that, in the end, if God exists, his reality must determine and control our theology. The fundamental hypothesis to be tested in theology by both believer and unbeliever in dialogue is whether critical investigation of the alleged media of divine–human encounter yields an objective and plausible view of God and the world.

Criticism is the chief mark of modern Christian

The problems of theology

theology, and it is likely that every religious tradition sooner or later will have increasingly to adopt consistently self-critical methods. In Christian theology they have been applied for a long time now to the scriptures and to the historical traditions of Christianity, including, more recently, its whole doctrinal system. It is the great merit of Wolfhart Pannenberg in modern German theology to have insisted against Karl Barth (and against the existentialist theologian Rudolf Bultmann) that faith itself cannot be excluded from scrutiny, and that its rational basis in conviction must be examined publicly.

It follows that, apart from maintaining his overall intention to scrutinise the Christian tradition in all its aspects for its ability to mediate knowledge of God, man and the universe, the Christian theologian has no single method. Critical methods are diverse and they are the common property of philosophers, historians and students of ancient texts as well as theologians. Their application in theology will be illustrated and discussed in subsequent chapters. Only the refusal to stop short of the quest for ultimate truth and meaning and the refusal to reject the possibility of divine revelation differentiate the theologian from his colleagues.

There has been much discussion of theological method in recent years. The influential Roman Catholic theologian Bernard Lonergan has set out an eightfold pattern of methodical approaches in theology, within a fourfold set of general principles for any disciplined enquiry.* No one will quarrel with the general principles: be attentive, be intelligent, be reasonable, be responsible. There is also a great deal of insight to be gained from the eight methodical approaches which Lonergan distinguishes. I shall not go through them here. I

* B. Lonergan, *Method in Theology* (London: Darton, Longman and Todd, 1972).

mention them only in order to make two points against Lonergan. Firstly, however illuminating a detailed account of method in theology such as Lonergan's may be, it is unlikely that a single programme worked out by an individual author will succeed in specifying *the* method in theology. Within the overall intention to think through the total world-view that has come down to us in each religious tradition, any and every critical method must be tried out and pursued as far as it will go. We cannot prescribe a single pattern.

Secondly, we are bound to question Lonergan's insistence on the role of religious conversion at a certain stage in his eightfold programme. For Lonergan the higher reaches of theology can be attained only on the basis of a religious conversion which gives the theologian the necessary perspective or 'horizon' within which to think theologically. This reliance on 'conversion', like the reliance on 'faith' which we discussed earlier, renders theological judgements undiscussable across the borders of the different world religions. On this aspect of Lonergan's method, Wolfhart Pannenberg has written: 'the alternative to that way in modern theology has been to let theology be discussed without reservations in the context of critical rationality'.* The present writer endorses that alternative.

To insist on throwing theology open to such critical discussion involves no disparagement of living religious faith and no down-grading of its place in religion. On the contrary the simple faith of religious men and women, and the faith of believing theologians, are an essential part of the data on which theology must work. Moreover it may very well be the case that, for many people, some sort of conversion or opening of the eyes to a new vision of reality is a necessary condition of religious faith. But

* P. Corcoran (ed.), *Looking at Lonergan's Method* (Dublin: Talbot Press, 1975), p. 98.

The problems of theology

neither conversion nor faith is a necessary condition of theological thinking. The theologian working from within does not possess an unassailable and undiscussable vantage point. To suppose that he does is to buy security at too high a cost. It lifts theology out of the sphere of rational discussion and leads to the absurd claim that theological rationality has its own private logic. There is no such thing as a private logic. Naturally the actual content of religious belief in God, if true, will demand self-involvement. But there are degrees of involvement, and there are degrees of sympathetic understanding across the borders of the religions and of belief and unbelief.

These remarks on theological method are controversial. But the fact that Christian theology has increasingly to be studied in a world wide context, and with a constant eye upon the question of a theology of the world religions, must surely reinforce this plea for an open, self-critical approach in theology. One of the most interesting problems in theology today is the question how far each religion can permit and foster such an approach. A rough and ready survey might lead one to suppose that Hindu theology is well placed to carry it out; Christian theology has in fact pursued it furthest so far (though not without strenuous internal opposition); Jewish theology has not shown very much interest in it; and Muslim theology has shown the strongest resistance to it. Only the future can show the degree to which each tradition can and will adopt the critical methods advocated here. Equally only the future can show the fruitfulness of such approaches.

The task of theology

The prime task of theology is that of understanding. What makes a man or a woman a theologian is first and foremost the desire to know the truth about his or her re-

20

ligion or that of other people. To that end the theologian has to try to set aside both pietistic and apologetic motives. He is not primarily concerned, *qua* theologian, to deepen faith or to defend a gospel.

It has already been admitted that, if God exists, the reality with which the theologian is concerned will inevitably be discovered to involve practical claims and consequences. Some of these are discussed in Chapter 7. It will also be discovered, no doubt, that God, if he exists, is to be worshipped and adored. But it is one thing to pray to God, another to exercise clear and critical thought upon the problems of theology.

Marxist–Leninists have claimed, and some men of religion, particularly Christians, have agreed with them, that our task is not to understand or interpret the world but to change it. No doubt the world needs to be changed, and theological studies may well contribute to perception of that need and of the resources available for the transformation of men and women and of their societies. But to set the task of change over against that of understanding is not only foolish but disastrous. It could be urged that it is because they have *not* understood the world that Marxist–Leninists have precipitated rapid social change at the cost of untold human suffering and with very mixed results, including harsh totalitarianism.

To return to the case of Christian theology, something should be said about its function *vis-à-vis* the Christian Church. If the prime task of theology is understanding, there must be a certain distancing from the direct concerns of the churches. Admittedly the believing theologian will want his search for truth to yield results for the faith and liturgy and practice of the Church, not least in its preaching and its mission. Equally the Christian Church will be well-advised to make its faith and order, life and work more theologically informed. But from the theologian's point of view, these results are secondary. The believing theologian cannot commit his unbelieving

21

The problems of theology

or less believing colleagues to these enterprises, nor can he allow his own commitment to them to interfere with his quest for understanding and his testing of the truth-claims of Christianity and other faiths. Moreover, these secondary tasks are specifically *not* part of the theologian's task in the university.

Theology and comparative religion

In this and the next chapter, we are to take further our discussion of the difference between theology and religious studies. Religious studies include both the comparative study of religions and the so-called scientific study of religion. We reserve the latter – the approaches of psychology, anthropology and sociology – for the next chapter, concentrating here on comparative religion. Our purpose is not to give a detailed account of its methods and aims, but rather to examine its claim both to be objective and to understand its data. We shall then discuss the relation between theology and comparative religion, examining each from the other's point of view. Finally we shall consider the vexed question of criteria of truth in the comparative study of religion.

The phenomenology of religion

In an attempt to look at the world of religion in all its fulness, without presupposing commitment to any particular religious beliefs, scholars have developed a discipline known as the phenomenology of religion. Indeed the phenomenological method may be thought of as the characteristic method of the comparative study of religion. This term 'phenomenology' has a long history in philosophy, but it is borrowed particularly from the German philosopher, Edmund Husserl (1859–1938), who used it for an allegedly presuppositionless approach to things simply as they appear in human consciousness. The method involves bracketing off all questions of truth and reality. Husserl claimed that, if one concentrates on appearances (phenomena) in all their fulness, one will be able to grasp intuitively the essence of whatever topic is under discussion. Applied to religion, this method involves bracketing off ultimate questions about God, and concentrating simply on the human phenomena of religious practice, experience and belief the world over. Then, from a comparative survey of the data, it is suggested, the observer will come to understand the essential nature of the different aspects of religion and, it may be hoped, of human religion as such.

From a purely descriptive point of view, this seems to be an excellent approach. Clearly the student of religion needs to know what he is talking about and to have as much detailed information about the whole world of religion before him as possible. Clearly, too, he needs some technique of appreciating the significance of all this material, of getting on the inside of it, as it were, and seeing what it meant or means to those involved. Since he is studying a large number of religions, past and present, he cannot himself be a participant in them all. Even if he *is* a religious believer, he can be a serious participant in only one religion, and so, in order to study comparative religion, he must learn to stand back from his own commitment and project himself imaginatively into that of other people. Similarly the uncommitted student will need to project himself imaginatively and sympathetically into the faith-world of those whose practices, experiences and beliefs he is studying. The phenomenology of religion encourages the student to think it possible to suspend belief or disbelief, to put on one side the question of truth, and to enter into the religious world as it presents itself to the careful observer. It is not a matter of purely external observation, as though the student were simply describing rituals and classifying institutions and practices. His careful observation extends to the inner world of those whom he is studying. To borrow a helpful example from Ninian Smart, he appreciates the fact that a Christian Eucharist finds its 'focus' in the risen Christ.* This is what the participants believe, and their feelings while taking part in a Eucharist are determined by that belief. The observer can understand all this, irrespective of his own beliefs and of the question whether Christ is really present in a Christian Eucharist. That question is bracketed off by the phenomenologist.

Another merit of phenomenological description is that, by presenting the religious phenomenon in its fulness, it discourages hasty judgements about what is really going on in the world of religion. As we shall see, students of religion have an inordinate tendency to bring to their work some prior theory of what religion is, or of what is really going on in some religious institution or practice. These theories, whether openly admitted or unconsciously assumed, will tend to colour the way the data are handled. Often the facts are twisted to fit the theory. But the phenomenological method helps us to resist this tendency. By suspending the whole problem of truth and reality, we let the facts – the phenomenal facts, that is – speak for themselves. Often, when we do this, some theory of religion is shown up quite clearly as false to the facts and guilty of what, to adapt a phrase of Winston Churchill's, we might call 'phenomenological inexactitude'.

So far so good. But the phenomenology of religion claims to be more than just a descriptive discipline. The trained sympathetic observer does not just describe. He selects, orders and classifies his material. The botanist does not just describe one flower after another. He classifies them according to their species and their wider family relationships. Similarly in the study of religion, the phenomenologist is bound to try to sort out his vast mass of material and introduce some order into his work.

* N. Smart, *The Phenomenon of Religion* (London: Macmillan, 1973), pp. 53ff.

Further, it is claimed that as soon as one carries out comparative work and begins to see the similarities in form and content of the different practices and beliefs in the different religions of the world, one begins to understand religion and to grasp its essential nature.

This is much more problematic. Of course there are similarities to be noted. For a start, we have to have some broad idea of what is to count as a religious phenomenon in the first place. There must be some means, however rough and ready, of picking out the religious from the non-religious.* Nor is it necessarily misleading to introduce very broad formal distinctions, as Ninian Smart does when he points out that most religions include rituals, myths, doctrines, ethical teachings, institutional or communal forms and special kinds of experience. This sixfold typology of dimensions of religion can be very helpful towards classifying the data and seeing the comparable role which different elements play in the life of each religion. The distinctions are sufficiently broad and formal not to distort the diverse material under consideration.

It is also possible to make more substantial distinctions, as Tillich does when he distinguishes between prophetic and mystical religion, or as Smart himself does when he distinguishes the mystical, the numinous and the incarnational strands running through a number of the world religions. It is clear that claims to mystical union with the divine or with ultimate reality do occur, to different degrees, in most major religions; it is clear that in many faiths men feel themselves to be confronted by an awesome yet demanding presence over against themselves; and it is also clear that a number of religions, in different ways, include beliefs that God or the gods have come amongst mankind in human form. These

---

* See J. Holm, *The Study of Religions* (London: Sheldon Press, 1977).

recurring features are much more debatable than the six formal dimensions of religion which Smart distinguished earlier. Scholars disagree, for example, as to whether there are different basic types of mystical experience or whether it is fundamentally the same experience interpreted differently in different contexts of belief. Again, scholars differ over the importance of these recurring features of religion. Rudolf Otto, who introduced the notion of the 'numinous' in his book *The Idea of the Holy*,* thought that the experience which he was stressing – what I paraphrased as experience of 'an awesome yet demanding presence' over against one – constituted the essence of religion, a unique mode of human awareness which made religion the thing it is. This is a highly questionable thesis. Not only are there other features to be noticed in the world of religious experience. It is far from clear that felt experience is the most important aspect of religion anyway, even if it is construed, as by Otto, as yielding knowledge of ultimate reality. Smart's third strand, the incarnational strand, is also a very debatable one. To lump together the Christian doctrine of the incarnation and the Hindu teaching about divine Avatārs who manifest God in human form to rescue men whenever evil prevails may obscure important differences and lead to superficial assimilation.†

This problem gets worse the more particular and precise the classificatory pigeon-holes become, into which the scholar sorts the beliefs and practices of the religions. The basic forms and strands which Tillich and Smart distinguish are still pretty broad, but when we turn to one of the classic studies in the phenomenology of religion, Gerardus van der Leeuw's *Religion in Essence and Mani-*

---

* London: OUP, 1923, and Harmondsworth: Penguin Books, 1959.
† See below, pp. 150–6.

The problems of theology

festation,* we find a large number of much more detailed categories – the sacrament, the medicine-man, the priest, sacrifice, the sacred word and so on – into which examples from the different religions are slotted, all allegedly illustrating the common structure and nature of religion.

This kind of 'typological phenomenology' is in grave danger of distorting the facts. Wolfhart Pannenberg has pointed out how unhistorical it is. It classifies together many different examples, irrespective of time or place or of the stage of development which a particular phenomenon has reached in the history of the religion in question. And it has no means whatsoever, Pannenberg argues, of distinguishing deep and important common structures from superficial similarities. It may constitute a method of handling and sorting the vast amount of material for study which the religions provide, but it gives us no basis for understanding the data. Indeed it may positively mislead.

However, the phenomenology of religion is not restricted to this kind of typological classification. As Smart has urged, a properly *historical* phenomenology can take account of the full context and development of the features of each religion. To understand the Christian Eucharist, it is much more important to study the Jewish Passover, the passion of Jesus and what the growing Christian churches made of his death and resurrection (according to their strong conviction) than to compare sacramental meals in other religions. For historical phenomenology, comparative religion is a matter of noting contrasts and differences more than similarities.

These considerations take us back to the idea that the phenomenology of religion is primarily a descriptive study. As the last paragraph showed, it enables us to understand the data only in relation to the particular,

* English trans., London: Allen and Unwin, 1938, and New York: Harper and Row (Harper Torchbooks edition), 1963.

historically shaped, framework of beliefs of those involved. Attempts to go further and speak of a common structure or universal essence of religion are highly dubious undertakings. Either one tends to make too much of superficial similarities that may strike the casual observer, or one imports into one's study some prior theory of what religion is. Nevertheless as a descriptive discipline, phenomenology remains a useful approach. It trains us to observe carefully and to take account of the wide range of religious data. We learn to see the practices and beliefs of different peoples in their context and to note differences as well as apparently common elements.

Objectivity in the comparative study of religion

There may well still be some doubts in readers' minds about the phenomenological method just described. How can it really be objective if it brackets off questions of truth and reality before it starts? Admittedly one might think that one was being objective in one's study of religion, if, given the widespread disagreements over the very being, let alone the nature of God, one adopted a neutral stance and studied people's beliefs and feelings, irrespective of the truth or falsity of what they believe. Compare the historian. Is he not being objective when he studies a political controversy in the past without taking sides? He expounds both points of view together with the reasons advanced on both sides, indicates certain factors influencing the participants in their adoption of their views, and shows what came of the dispute. Is that not a model of objectivity for the student of religion to follow?

The trouble with this comparison is that the question of reality, of what was and is really going on in the history of religion, is not strictly parallel to the question of evaluation which divides political opponents. Of course, one side in the political controversy may have been disastrously wrong, and the historian will hardly have done his job if he fails to point this out. But even so, to study political disagreement 'objectively' is not really comparable to studying religion 'objectively'. For to treat religion as a purely human phenomenon like politics is already, according to one party in the dispute, to abstract from the full reality in question. Certainly one can study religion as a purely human phenomenon, and it is doubtless an instructive thing to do, but it is to do something different from studying politics as a purely human phenomenon. For politics *is* a purely human phenomenon and all are agreed that it is, whereas religion's status as a purely human phenomenon is in dispute.

In Chapter 1 we discussed the notion of a proper objectivity, that is, an objectivity appropriate to the reality in question. We saw that the mark of genuine science is letting the object itself, whatever we are studying, determine and control our knowing. The aim of science is to get at the real facts, not just the appearances, and certainly not to treat the facts as something other than what they really are. The very distinction between appearance and reality was introduced, early in the history of philosophy, precisely because it was realised that appearances can mislead. So a method which deliberately sticks to appearances, just because the reality is disputed and hard to get, is not likely to win prizes for 'objectivity' in this deeper sense.

The phenomenologist might reply that perhaps people are too hasty in their eagerness to get at reality. Did not Husserl invent the method because philosophers were so divided on the nature of reality? Idealists asserted that absolute spirit alone is ultimately real; empiricists asserted that only the data of sense can provide a sure foundation for human knowledge. Yet we all live in the same world. Perhaps a closer attention to the way things appear to human beings and are registered in human consciousness will prevent us from making over-hasty assertions about reality. And maybe it is only superficially noted appearances that have a tendency to mislead. Maybe patient and disciplined attention to the way things appear will prove a surer path to the knowledge of reality after all. On such a view, the phenomenological bracketing of questions of truth and reality is only a temporary, provisional step. Later on, when the careful descriptions have been made, we may be in a better position to 'return reality to the world'. Certainly Husserl thought so, and some of his successors in existentialist philosophy made it their intention right from the start to let being – reality itself – come into focus in and through sustained attention to our own human consciousness of being and acting in the world.

Applied to the case of religion, a similar line of argument could be constructed. Theists assert that God is real and active. Atheists assert the opposite. May it not be the case that a disciplined investigation of how things appear to the human religious consciousness the world over is a necessary preliminary step to a more surely based discovery of truth and reality in religion?

This view has some claim to be taken seriously. But for two reasons it still does not succeed in resolving our doubts about the phenomenology of religion. For one thing, the majority of students of religion do not in fact adopt the phenomenological method as a useful preparatory step before moving on to the question of truth. On the contrary they bracket the question of truth in order to be able to study religion without having to answer the really difficult questions. But if religion is treated just as a purely human phenomenon, then the abstraction which this involves can quickly be forgotten, and suspension of judgement on the issue of truth can become, in Pannenberg's words, 'a prejudice in favour of an immanent or anthropological interpretation of religion'.*

* W. Pannenberg, *Theology and the Philosophy of Science*, English trans. (London: Darton, Longman and Todd, 1976), p. 363.

The problems of theology

In the second place, even if the phenomenological 'bracketing' is only a temporary step, intended to prepare the ground for a more informed attempt to grapple with the question of religious truth, it still begs a number of questions to suppose that this is the best or only way of getting at the truth. Admittedly it *may* be the case that God's reality is mediated to mankind through the religious consciousness, in which case study of the religious consciousness is indeed a good place to begin. But whether that is so or not is a question for the philosopher and for the theologian. We shall see in Chapters 4 and 5 that there are very different views on where we are to look for intimations of the divine.

It will be readily apparent from this discussion that the problem of objectivity in the study of religion is an extremely tricky one. If we attempt to be objective in the neutral sense of suspending judgement and just surveying the whole disputed field of man's religion, we are liable to beg the question against the reality of God. If, however, we attempt to be objective in the sense of letting our minds conform to what is really going on in the world of religion, we are liable to be accused of begging the question the other way, and requiring the student of religion to become a believing theologian. Perhaps this problem can be best resolved by adopting the open understanding of theology which we defended in Chapter 1. On that view, the theologian is not someone who is necessarily committed to belief in God. He is rather someone for whom the question of God is an important and open one. In this sense of theology, it can be argued that the comparative study of religion does point us on in the direction of theology. In a word, the facts of religion raise the question of God.

I should like to conclude these reflections on the problem of objectivity by returning to the question whether one's own religious experience or lack of it is a help or a hindrance to one's study of comparative religion. The usual analogies suggested are much too simple. An unbeliever studying religion, it is said, is like a blind man studying painting or a tone-deaf man studying music. One can see the point of such analogies, but one can also see that they imply that religious awareness is a single unique faculty, which one either possesses or does not possess. That is a very large assumption.

In fact religious believers are very complex creatures. They live within certain traditions of belief and practice, and they share certain characteristic attitudes fostered by their religion. But their thinking and their feeling are not of one standard type nor is their specifically religious awareness cut off and isolated from their personal relations and attitudes in general. Love of God is not, for the believer, something totally different from love of other human beings. Christianity, for example, teaches that all human love is an image of and participation in the divine love, and that a man's conception of the divine love is by analogy with human love. Consequently it is not impossible for someone who has experienced human love to imagine what it is like to experience one's life as something personally given and to love God as the source of one's being.

Moreover there are some people who used to believe but no longer do so, or who used not to believe but now do. Others have moments when they experience the world religiously and moments when they do not. These experiences can be discussed and shared. Any sympathetic and imaginative person can enter into them, at least to some extent. Across the borders of the different religions, the matter is complicated by the different historical and cultural contexts of belief. But one can come to understand at least something of quite different religious traditions just as one can study great literature from widely differing times and places. Now one does not have to write poetry oneself in order to understand it, though one requires a certain sensitivity and flexibility of mind, as well as hard work, especially if the poem comes from an ancient or distant culture.

The fact is that one's own belief and experience may or may not be a help. Someone who holds strongly that his own religion is the only true religion and that all other forms of religion are idolatry and sin will be less well placed to study, say, tribal religion in Africa or the different forms of Hinduism than the sensitive and open-minded agnostic. Equally someone who believes that all religion is nonsense will make a poor student of any religion. It is more important in religious studies to possess a sensitive imagination and a serious interest in religion than to be a man of religion oneself. On the other hand it is asking a lot of a man who has never been inclined himself to be religious to show that sensitivity and interest. On balance it is probably true to say that, given sensitivity and interest and provided one maintains a critical mind and a readiness to learn from others, some experience of religion from the inside is more of a help than a hindrance in religious studies.

Theology and comparative religion – co-operation or conflict?

The relationship between comparative religion and theology is by no means a straightforward one. In comparative religion we are looking at a wide variety of religious traditions, stretching back over thousands of years, most of which, though not all, have claimed to foster knowledge of God. They have done so in very different and often conflicting ways. Each major theistic tradition has given rise to its own theology or theologies, and one's first reaction is to think of these theologies as simply one among many sets of religious phenomena to be observed.

But, as we have seen, the actual facts which one comes across in studying religions, their claims to be dealing with ultimate reality and man's total situation in the universe, their claims to enshrine some insight into or revelation of the meaning of life and the ultimate future of man, are facts which will not lie down quietly under scrutiny. They cry out for some answer to the question, True or false? The question arises, Who is in a position to hazard an answer? Is it the student of comparative religion himself? Is it the psychologist or anthropologist or sociologist? Is it perhaps the philosopher? Or is it none of these, but rather the theologian after all?

The student of comparative religion as such is in no position to give an answer. We have just been looking at his difficulties. If he adopts the phenomenological method, he suspends judgement and deliberately gives no answer. If he comes down from his phenomenological perch into the hurly-burly of the dispute, as his subject matter inevitably invites him to do, he is bound to become more than just a student of comparative religion. He must himself become a psychologist, anthropologist, sociologist, philosopher or theologian. The first four possibilities will be considered later. Here we are considering the problems involved in his becoming a theologian.

The obvious problem is partiality. It looks, from his own study of religion, as if it is not possible to become a theologian in general. He must either become a Christian theologian or a Muslim theologian or a Hindu theologian, etc. Even if he accepts our earlier open definition of theology as dialogue between believer and unbeliever over the question of God, it looks as if he would have to undertake this dialogue from within the confines of a particular religion. Certainly one cannot be a believer in general – or if one can, one's position is likely to be far too vague to yield much in the way of theology. There is little serious religious alternative to being a Christian or a Muslim or a Hindu, etc. There have been attempts to foster a syncretistic faith, calling upon insights from all the world religions, but in so far as they have survived at all they have always become separate faiths, each requiring its own theology – if they ever develop that far.

The suggestion has recently been made, however, that in these days of global intercommunication, it is possible for each religion's theology to become a wider and more all-embracing affair than the religion itself. This view is urged by the English philosopher of religion John Hick.* For Hick, it is possible, indeed necessary, for the Christian theologian, while remaining religiously a Christian in his own faith and worship, to transcend his own standpoint theologically, by seeing his own tradition as one concrete embodiment in a particular historical and cultural context of the divine–human encounter, which takes different forms in different strands of human history. From the standpoint of India, the Hindu theologian could and should make a similar move.

This is an attractive suggestion for our student of comparative religion, wondering how to tackle the question of religious truth, raised for him by the phenomena of religion. In so far as he is himself a believer he will maintain his own religious affiliation but go beyond it theologically in constructing and testing a global theology of religion and the religions. In so far as he is not a believer, he will go straight to the global theology and investigate its grounds and rationality, in dialogue with those approaching the questions from within their various traditions.

The trouble with this suggestion is that it is itself liable to fall foul of the actual data of religion. The student of religion is bound to ask himself whether Hick's global theology does not suffer from 'phenomenological inexactitude' in that the claimed insights or revelations

* *God and the Universe of Faiths* (London: Macmillan, 1973), chs. 9 and 10.

of the different world religions would have to be denied before such a global theology could be accepted. If so, the global theology would no longer involve a theological harmonisation of the religious history of man. It would become just one suggestion among others, really a philosophical alternative to the actual theologies which the religions themselves can sustain.

Nevertheless the idea that, in looking to theology for a possible answer to the question of truth in religion, one must require each religion's theologians to include an explanation of the whole fact of religion and of what is going on in the other religions of the world is an inescapable factor in theology today. The student of religion in turning to the theologian (or in becoming a theologian) is entitled to demand of the latter how he relates his alleged Christian (or Muslim or Hindu) truth-claims to the experience and beliefs of other faiths. And the theologian cannot avoid taking note of those data to which the student of comparative religion calls his attention.

The fact that, unless Hick's global theology is right, the student of comparative religion will now be confronted with a number of rival theologies of religion, each claiming to answer the question of religious truth and to comprehend each other's answers, should lead us to consider the possibility of comparative theology, in which reflective, critical participants in each tradition put forward their systematic understanding of God, man and the universe, including their understanding of each other. The student of religion will want to participate in this discussion and to join in testing, so far as he can, the adequacy of each view.

Comparative theology is not just another aspect of the comparative study of religion, however. For, as we have seen, if God does exist, then the knowledge of God which is fostered in the religions and formulated in their theologies may well involve the student of religion in a transfer of attention from religion to God. The possibility, at any rate, exists that the 'objectivity' of his phenomenological suspense of judgement will have to yield to intellectual assent to the objectivity of God. Equally, of course, the possibility exists that the theologian's alleged understanding of God and his relation to the world will turn out to be a baseless construction. In which case he would have to retreat from his claimed theological objectivity back to what would have turned out to be the more appropriate phenomenological objectivity of the student of comparative religion.

Criteria of truth in religion

In Chapters 3 and 4, consideration will be given to the possibility of alternative explanations, whether scientific or philosophical, of religious practices, experiences and beliefs. Here we stay with comparative theology and pursue the problem of truth in religion a little further. On the assumption that Hick's global theology is impossible and that there are genuinely conflicting truth-claims between the religions, the question immediately arises, What are the criteria by which the truth or greater degree of truth of any one religious or theological view might be established? This is the most important as well as the most difficult question facing anyone who undertakes the task of comparative theology. We have already seen that any particular theology from within a particular religion must, in addition to articulating its own internal tradition, attempt some account of the plurality of religions, each with its own rival theology. But what are the criteria for greater or greatest success in this whole enterprise?

Many people think that there are no such criteria, since each participant in comparative theology from within a particular religion is bound to be biased in favour of his own account, and no neutral observer is in a position to judge between the rival accounts. This very natural view may, however, be premature. It is worth at least considering possible criteria that have been suggested in books on comparative theology. And if what was said in Chapter 1 about the possibility of doing theology hypothetically is taken seriously, then it may, after all, be possible for the uncommitted, yet sympathetic observer to reach the conclusion that one participant, say, in inter-faith dialogue, is doing a better job and making better sense than another.

Two writers in particular have given some attention to this problem – William A. Christian and Ninian Smart.* Christian first shows, painstakingly and clearly, that, whatever common elements may be discerned, there are genuinely incompatible proposals for belief coming out of the different world religions. He next sketches what he calls a model dialogue situation, in which informed and sane representatives of different religions meet to put forward and give reasons for some characteristic doctrines of their respective faiths. We may, perhaps, in the light of our earlier considerations, enlarge upon this model dialogue situation a little. We should insist that it is not just a question of each representative arguing for 'some characteristic doctrines' of his faith. He will need to present a rounded picture of his faith's theology, not only in its inner interconnections, but also in relation to our modern scientific knowledge of the world, and to the facts of religion and the history of religions the world over. His theology, in other words, will need to be both

---

* See W. A. Christian, *Meaning and Truth in Religion* (Princeton University Press, 1964), and *Oppositions of Religious Doctrines* (London: Macmillan, 1972); N. Smart, *Reasons and Faiths* (London: Routledge and Kegan Paul, 1958), *A Dialogue of Religions* (London: SCM Press, 1960), and *The Yogi and the Devotee* (London: Allen and Unwin, 1968).

systematic in itself and to include an interpretation of the whole world of religion. William Christian suggests that, among the participants in the model dialogue situation, we may include converts from one religion to another, who may speak to what they have found in their new faith which they did not find in their old one. We ourselves will also wish to include some sympathetic unbelievers and half-believers, prepared to entertain the various proposals hypothetically.

Christian points out that, in such a model dialogue situation, appeals to the authority of particular alleged sources of revelation are out of place. For there are no such agreed authorities between the participants.* If there are criteria of judgement here they must be general criteria, common to all participants in the model dialogue situation. This is what makes the question of criteria so difficult; for it is far from being agreed that there are any general common criteria which theologians from different religious traditions might appeal to, once one has moved from beliefs held in common to genuinely incompatible claims. Nevertheless, the attempt has been made, particularly by Smart, to suggest a number of possible criteria that might commend themselves as fulfilling this role. In the nature of the case they are 'soft' criteria. We are not to expect clear-cut, knock-down arguments here.

We may mention seven such criteria:

1 Coherence

It is necessary for any religious view of the world to be both internally coherent and coherent with all our other knowledge. It is incumbent upon an apologist for a particular religious position to show its inner rationality and also to show how it can be developed in ways compatible

---

* On this problem, see Chapter 5.

with scientific and historical knowledge, including knowledge of the history of religions. Otherwise he will be at a grave disadvantage in our model dialogue situation. Of course coherence by itself will not get us very far. No major religion is likely to be easily convicted of incoherence.

2 Simplicity

Smart mentions this as the criterion by which the religions are driven towards a unified view, whether monist or monotheist, as opposed to uncoordinated polytheistic faiths. One might well think that simplicity (or economy) is a dangerous criterion. On the principle known as 'Occam's razor' – entities are not to be multiplied without necessity – it might be thought to rule out religion (or at least the transcendent) altogether. But it is a mistake to consider the criterion of simplicity in isolation or solely in conjunction with coherence. It requires to be balanced by considerations of comprehensiveness.

3 Comprehensiveness

Part of the strength of a religious view of the world lies in its ability to make sense of all the data of experience and history. A participant in the model dialogue situation would be at a disadvantage if his religion had nothing to say about a central strand in human experience, religious or otherwise. Of course, it might be argued that to value comprehensiveness is already to favour one set of religious traditions rather than another, say those of early Buddhism. The Buddha apparently thought it religiously improper and self-defeating to dabble in metaphysical questions. But it is one thing to single out the all-important key to the problem of human existence; it is another to ignore whole dimensions of human life. It is sometimes held that later Buddhism developed more recognisably devotional forms just because an essential element in the religious experience of man had at first

The problems of theology

been left out. Ninian Smart has an interesting argument along these lines when he suggests that it is a point in favour of devotional faith that it can embrace the mystical strand in religion more easily than pure mysticism can embrace personal religion.

4 Ethical and spiritual profundity

Something will be said about comparative ethics in Chapter 7. It is undoubtedly hard to give reasons in support of different ethical and spiritual ideals; but at least it can be said that some commend themselves for their range and depth and moral creativity more than others. We are touching here on a criterion which is often best not put into words. It is a matter of action and character speaking louder than words. This indicates, of course, a limitation on our model *dialogue* situation. Similarly, it is very hard for believing theologians to make fair assessments of the moral and spiritual profundity of the founders and the saints of other religions. But there is no doubt that these factors play an important part in the way in which a particular faith commends itself.

5 Ability to cope with boundary situations

One of the functions of religion discerned by many sociologists of religion is that of sustaining a sense of meaning despite the problems of evil, suffering and death that threaten human existence. Participants in our model dialogue situation will wish to compare and discuss the ways in which their respective faiths have enabled men and women to account for, cope with and ultimately transcend these boundary situations.

6 Historical considerations

Some religions, especially Christianity, appeal very definitely to certain facts of history, as both eliciting and substantiating their claims. We shall see in Chapter 5 how Christianity locates divine revelation in certain very particular historical events. There will, of course, be disputes over the value and significance of history. This criterion, it must be admitted, is not so common and general as those already mentioned. Yet the life and death and, it is sometimes argued (at least in some respects), the resurrection of Jesus Christ are public facts in the public world, which, to say the least, must be allowed to carry some weight in the dialogue situation.

7 *The aesthetic criterion*

This is a phrase of Smart's by which he intends to refer to the way all these elements fit together and illuminate each other in each particular, developing and creative religious tradition.

Such are some of the considerations to which appeal might be made in the model dialogue situation. It will be noted that appeals to experience are not included in this list. That is because every religion fosters a certain kind of religious experience, and no religion can begin to win assent if it lacks the power to evoke a deep sense of devotion, meaning, stillness or ecstasy. No doubt these experiences will, as far as is possible, be mentioned and discussed in dialogue; but it is difficult to see how they can settle questions of truth. Comparative theology is bound to concern itself primarily with the interpretative rather than the experiential element in religion.

3

Theology, psychology and the social sciences

In turning to the more strictly scientific study of religion, we need to bear in mind that for the theologian the approaches of psychology, anthropology and sociology may turn out to be allies or they may turn out to be enemies.

They are enemies only if they are used to advance complete explanatory theories of religion, on the assumption that religion is a purely human phenomenon and nothing more. Convinced of the illusory nature of the alleged object of religion and theology, namely, God, the student may retreat for a time back to the neutral territory of the phenomenology of religion. But, if the arguments of the last chapter were correct, he cannot hope fully to understand and explain religion from the phenomenological standpoint alone. The question of truth remains, and if theological attempts to answer it have been rejected, then the student will have to look elsewhere. He may look to psychology or sociology for a complete explanation of the origin and nature of religion. In doing so, he is indicating his disillusion with theology and his conviction that religion is nothing but a human phenomenon. What he can not do is have his cake and eat it, that is, claim that he is looking for a *complete* explanation of religion *in so far as* it is a human phenomenon. That is a self-contradictory aim. No one can hedge his bets like that and talk of complete explanations at the same time.

Psychology, anthropology and sociology are the theologian's allies, however, if these disciplines are used to study and explain certain *aspects* of religion. The sciences of man have a great deal to say about such subjects as the way in which children acquire and develop religious ideas or the way in which social organisation and attitudes condition religious practice at different times and places. The psychological or sociological constraints upon an individual's concept of God, say, in South Africa today are important factors in the religious situation there. But the fact that there are such constraints does not necessarily exclude a man from some knowledge of God, if God is real, though they may distort both his religious awareness and his theological understanding. The theologian is likely to agree that the divine–human encounter takes place through the media of institutions and beliefs which have a discoverable history and intelligible interrelations with each other and with the rest of the social environment. To study these aspects of religion and to become aware of these conditioning factors, far from inhibiting theology, should serve to free it from hidden bondage to unknown causal processes. That is why the human sciences can be allies of theology, once the limits of their scope are recognised.

Psychology and theology

The aim of the psychology of religion is to study the formation and development of religious ideas and feelings in the individual. Unless this is being done in the interests of some reductive theory of religion, the investigation will leave open the question of the degree to which the ideas and feelings under scrutiny can be the vehicles of knowledge of God.

One of the pioneers in the psychology of religion was the American philosopher and psychologist, William James (1842–1910). In his *The Varieties of Religious Experience* he studied phenomena such as conversion and mysticism with a view to determining what factors make a man prone to such experiences and whether different kinds of religious experience are correlated with different psychological types of human being. It is not surprising that the interest of James and many subsequent psychologists has focused on the mystical consciousness; for it stands out as a distinctive and recurring feature in the history of religions that some people achieve the most exalted states of consciousness, at once held to be beyond verbal description and at the same time referred to as oneness with nature, enlightenment, identity with Brahman, union with Allah or with Christ. Clearly these extraordinary states, whether or not they actually do involve awareness of and union with transcendent reality, are not entirely without connection with what has gone before in the mystic's mental life; nor of course are they without a physiological base in his brain activity. The fact that such states can be simulated by certain drugs can tell us something of the underlying mechanics of mysticism (though one needs to remember that the fact that under certain physiological conditions a man 'sees' non-existent pink rats does not mean that he is not really seeing pink rats when there *are* some around). Equally the psychologist, by studying a broad range of mystical writings from different religious traditions (by no means just theistic traditions), and by collecting reports from living mystics, will be able to show whether there are any connections between the incidence of mystical experience and other mental factors such as a proneness to hysteria. He will also have something to say about the dispute mentioned earlier as to whether there are fundamentally different forms of mystical experience or whether a common psychological state is construed differently in different contexts of belief. In all this the psychologist, like any other student, needs to avoid the temptation of jumping to conclusions. The view that 'the mystical ecstasies of the great mystics were really orgasms aroused in sexually deprived young women with hysterical temperaments' is liable to fall foul of the test of 'phenomenological exactitude' when applied, for example, to the life of the Buddha.

The psychologist of religion will naturally be interested in other abnormal religious phenomena such as the meditation techniques of Indian yoga, or the phenomenon of speaking with tongues associated with pentecostal or charismatic revivals. The fact that speaking with tongues in Christian congregations can be shown to be a comparable phenomenon to other ecstatic utterances in other religious groups, and the fact that a psychological account can be given of the way religious excitement can give rise to such non-rational outbursts, should make the theologian pause before endorsing the naive religious judgement that in speaking with tongues we have an immediate effect of the divine Spirit. That is without prejudice to the possibility that non-rational ecstatic enthusiasm *may* become the vehicle of genuine religious growth in a community. On the other hand there are psychological states, such as those alleged to manifest demon possession, which on theological grounds are best handed over entirely to the psychologist for explanation.*

However, abnormal states are by no means the only preoccupation of psychologists of religion. As was mentioned just now, the normal acquisition and assimilation of religious concepts in childhood and adolescence have been the object of much study by educational psychologists such as Jean Piaget in France and Ronald Goldman in England. It is clearly of great importance for religious educationists to know at what age a child is capable of understanding religious ideas. A further area of study is that of the temperamental differences that incline different people for or against a common tradition of religious belief. The study of the predisposition towards

* See B. L. Hebblethwaite, *Evil, Suffering and Religion* (London: Sheldon Press, 1976), pp. 45–8.

atheism is as important for both psychology and theology as is the study of the predisposition towards belief. Much of the kind of work in the psychology of religion is pretty humdrum. It involves the preparation of questionnaires and the careful tabulation of results.

The bearing of psychoanalysis and analytical psychology upon religion needs to be mentioned briefly here. The Austrian founder of psychoanalysis, Sigmund Freud (1856–1939), is notorious for his reductive account of religion as an illusion based on wish-fulfilment and of the idea of God as a projection of a father-figure on to the sky. For Freud, God is the illusory object of neurotic guilt feelings transferred from childhood 'Oedipal' feelings about a real father. These views are a typical example of the kind of theory of the origin and nature of religion that indicates a prior rejection of religion. Freud's theories of religion go way beyond the actual evidence of the case-histories of his patients. It is interesting that his more restricted psychoanalytic theory and practice can quite easily be used by Christian and other religious therapists within the context of belief. Thus the school known as 'clinical theology' uses Freud's methods in the cure of patients from neuroses which inhibit them from practising a mature Christianity; and perhaps more searchingly the theologian Harry Williams uses Freudian insights in the presentation of a theology of self-awareness. Thus Freudian psychoanalysis and theology can be allies. They become enemies only when a complete reductive theory of religion is superimposed upon the more basic understanding of neurosis and repression.

The Swiss analytical psychologist, Carl Gustav Jung (1875–1961), was much more sympathetic to religion, and recognised the importance of a religious outlook on life for the emotional health of the individual. Furthermore his theories of the collective unconscious and of the archetypal ideas that recur in human consciousness the world over have been found valuable in the study of religious symbolism. It should be noted that Jung's views on religion can be accepted irrespective of the truth or falsehood of any specific religious doctrines. Jung does not do the theologian's work for him, though the theologian can quite easily embrace the human wisdom of Jung's writings. Jung wisely refrained from offering an exhaustive theory of religion, thus leaving the theological options open.

Anthropology and theology

The borders between psychology, anthropology and sociology are blurred. Psychology's prime interest is in individual consciousness but the facts of group life and shared ideas demand the extension of the discipline into social psychology and the social sciences generally, as the example of Jung will already have indicated. Freud did not only offer a psychological theory of the origin of religion in the individual's childhood; he also propounded an anthropological theory (of even less merit) of the origin of religion in the childhood of the human race. Anthropology is often called social anthropology and it is only a convention that restricts anthropological interest to non-literate, so-called 'primitive' societies and sociological interest to modern developed societies. But both anthropology and sociology are concerned with the significance of religion in man's social life, and the effect of social structure and attitudes on the development of religions.

Religion is bound to feature prominently in anthropological studies, since it plays so central and pervasive a part in the lives of non-literate peoples. Nor is it surprising that in the nineteenth century, when anthropological studies began, there was a great deal of jumping to conclusions on very inadequate evidence about the origin of religion. The religions of non-literate tribes in Africa, North America and Australasia were held to have preserved religion at a very early stage in its evolution and to enable us to understand its origins in myths about great men, in ancestor cults or in what was called 'animism' – the attribution of personal spiritual power to regular or extraordinary natural forces. Much of this armchair theorising is worthless, as E. Evans-Pritchard has shown.* Alternatively, and more interestingly, the place of religion in the life of the tribe was held to show, in a relatively simple social system, the nature and function of religion generally as a unifying factor, both reflecting group solidarity and cementing the allegiance of each member to the way of life of his tribe. A notable example of this approach was Emile Durkheim's *Elementary Forms of the Religious Life*.

Durkheim, however, shared the nineteenth-century tendency to advance complete theories of religion. The implication was that, once one had seen the social function of religion in maintaining solidarity and something of the way it did so, there was no more to be said.

Modern anthropological study of religion is much more detailed and accurate and much more modest in its theoretical conclusions. The accuracy is achieved by long periods of field-work among particular tribes. A number of excellent studies have been published, such as Evans-Pritchard's *Nuer Religion*† and Godfrey Lienhardt's *Divinity and Experience: the Religion of the Dinka*.‡ Certainly the function of religion in these societies is brought out in such studies, but much more attention is paid to the meanings actually found in their rites by the participants themselves (thus exemplifying the phenomenological method described in the last chapter), and no exhaustive claims are made about such primitive religions being nothing but completely explicable human

* *Theories of Primitive Religion* (Oxford: Clarendon Press, 1965).

† Oxford: Clarendon Press, 1956.

‡ Oxford: Clarendon Press, 1961.

phenomena. Evans-Pritchard himself is explicit in leaving room for the theologian to offer his interpretation of the facts of primitive religion.

Mention has been made of the *function* of religion *vis-à-vis* the *structure* of tribal society. In such usage the term 'structure' is applied to the wider phenomenon of society, and religion is seen as an element in that structure. But anthropologists have also noted certain common structures in religious myths and rites themselves. This internal use of the term 'structure' is reflected in the approach of the French anthropologist, Lucien Lévi-Strauss, known as structuralism. Lévi-Strauss detects particularly in religious myths a deep, unconscious structure which reveals the way the human mind works in coming to terms with constant features of its environment. This theory has much in common with Jung's theory of archetypes, and can be regarded as neutral between theological and non-theological interpretation.

The importance of anthropology for theology lies in the fact that, once the theologian recognises the need to articulate a theology of religion and the religions, he will have to offer some theological account of primitive religion. He will suggest, perhaps, that its deep structure is best to be regarded as the dawning – and the consolidation (so far as close-knit non-literate communities permit) – of human consciousness of God. On this view its social function is a secondary one. Moreover the theologian may also suggest that the very fact that religion is so pervasive a feature of the human world, however far back in time we go and however widely we range through the surviving tribal societies, is an indication that some form of openness to the transcendent belongs to the essence of man. Dialogue between the theologian and the anthropologist will concern the possibility of such a theological anthropology.

The problems of theology

Sociology and theology

The figure of Emile Durkheim straddles the hazy border between social anthropology and sociology. He held that what elementary forms of religion illustrate most clearly of the unifying function of religion in society is true of all religion, even in the highly complex differentiated societies of the modern world. In so far as religion survives, it is to be interpreted as a mechanism for the achievement of consensus in society and as a symbolic representation of that ideal social harmony. The coronation of Queen Elizabeth II in Westminster Abbey in 1953 could be interpreted as a splendid illustration of Durkheim's thesis on the nature and function of religion. It was Durkheim, too, who insisted most strongly on the priority of sociological over psychological explanations. 'I consider extremely fruitful,' he wrote, 'this idea that social life should be explained, not by the notions of those who participate in it, but by more profound causes which are unperceived by consciousness, and I think also that these causes are to be sought mainly in the manner according to which the associated individuals are grouped.' This view has been strongly attacked, for instance by Peter Winch.* Winch points out that it is the notions of those who participate that make human activity and human society what they are. Social life is actually constituted by our own notions, concepts and meanings. Thus, to understand a religious practice or institution, we have to appreciate what it means to those taking part.

Our study of the phenomenological approach would lead us initially to support Winch against Durkheim. For if Durkheim is right it would be possible to say what is *really* going on in social life irrespective of what people

---

* See *The Idea of a Social Science* (London: Routledge and Kegan Paul, 1958), pp. 23–4.

think they are doing. Such a view of the universal oper-
ation of hidden causes is much too extreme. Nevertheless
it is probable that Winch goes too far in the opposite direction. For it does seem to be the case that human activity and human social life *in part* have hidden causes
unknown to the participants, and *in part* have unforeseen consequences. Thus it may be that a man's class in
part determines his political or religious views. And it
may be that the German sociologist, Max Weber (1864–
1920), was right in thinking that the Protestant work
ethic contributed to the rise of modern capitalism,*
though the sixteenth-century Puritans would have had
no idea that such a consequence would stem from their
religious attitudes.

It is reasonable, then, to think of the sociology of religion as the study of the hidden causes and unforeseen
consequences of religious forms of life. As we saw to be
the case with anthropology, the nineteenth- and early-
twentieth-century pioneers in the sociological study of
religion, such as Durkheim – and the same is true of Karl
Marx – tended to adopt complete explanatory theories
of religion, while their modern successors are much more
modest in restricting their attention to particular aspects
of religion in so far as they can be shown to exemplify a
typical pattern of cause and effect. The theologian has no
quarrel with this more modest approach. On the contrary he welcomes its ability to account for the variety
and partial nature of religious awareness.

Sociology, like psychology, can generalise only on the
basis of a wide range of evidence, and this involves the sociologist in a great deal of comparative work. Thus Max
Weber, having formulated his hypothesis about the
effect of the Protestant ethic on the rise of capitalism,
went on to study the religions of India and China, to see

---

* M. Weber, *The Protestant Ethic and the Spirit of Capitalism*,
English trans. (London: Allen and Unwin, 1930).

whether differences in religious attitudes there could account for the failure of those societies to develop capitalism. Weber was also responsible for the theory of 'ideal types', according to which individuals, relationships and attitudes can be examined for the degree to which they approximate to certain typical patterns. In his well-known study of charismatic leadership, Weber showed how, typically, a prophetic figure emerges in a time of crisis, wins a following by his gifts of leadership and inspiration, and creates a novel form of religious community, which after the first generation of support tends to fall back into a standard pattern of group organisation. The great merit of Weber's approach was that he realised that he was indicating only tendencies, not rigid laws. The sociologist, on this view, can predict only what is liable to happen, not what is bound to happen.

A great deal of illuminating sociological work has been done along these lines on the typical patterns of church life and attitudes, compared and contrasted with those of the sects, and on how both leaders and led see their roles in relation to each other and to the wider society.

One of the difficulties for the sociologist is the fact that his data keep changing. Unlike the natural scientist, he is not dealing with fixed quantities but with people and groups, which sometimes do unexpected and creative things. This serves to bring out the limitations of sociology. Whereas the theologian is interested in religious innovations, transformations and developments, the sociologist tends to be interested in factors making for equilibrium in society, and for standard patterns that reimpose themselves after a period of turbulence. One of the reasons why there are so many sociological studies of sectarian groups is that the sect tends to be a close-knit exclusive organisation, resisting change and development.

Nevertheless, increasingly we find sociological studies

of social and religious change. Much attention has recently been paid to the phenomenon of secularisation – the fact that, since the rise of modern science in the west, religion's hold on institutions and attitudes has steadily been eroded. We shall be discussing this example in the next section.

It is important to realise that if the sciences of man are dealing only with *aspects* of the human situation and with *tendencies* in individual and group life, then their descriptions and explanations are neither exclusive nor exhaustive – except in exceptional cases where a single factor becomes determinative, as in severe psychotic illness. Thus it was foolish of Durkheim to set sociological explanations over and above psychological explanations (as he did in his well-known study of suicide). Equally it is a mistake to try to reduce sociological concepts such as type, role, class and structure to psychological ones. Both have a place, and neither is (usually) exhaustive. Individuals certainly have typical wants and needs, and they certainly find themselves in typical social systems and processes. But, as the philosopher Karl Popper argues, while the fact that we are the products of our past and our context imposes some limits on what we can do, it also provides our critical and creative powers with material to work on and make something of. The theologian has an interest in preserving this balanced attitude to the scope and limits of the human sciences.

The sociology of knowledge

The theologian will be particularly interested in the sociological investigation of religious belief and of the different claims to knowledge of God that have formed an important part of the history of religions. He will resist the typical nineteenth-century attempts to explain away religious belief as nothing but fantasy and illusion (Marx and Freud) or a symbolic mode of representing

The problems of theology

and reinforcing society itself (Durkheim). He is bound to pay close attention, however, to more recent work in the sociology of knowledge, such as the pioneering work of Karl Mannheim* and Peter Berger's *The Social Reality of Religion*.†

At first sight, however, there seems to be something very odd about the very idea of the sociology of knowledge. The philosopher will be inclined to say that knowledge, if it is really knowledge, cannot be subject to explanation in terms of hidden causes. He will admit unforeseen consequences of human knowledge (such as economic ones), but knowledge is defined as *true* belief in circumstances where a man has a right and is in a position to know, and consequently talk of hidden causes is out of place. There will certainly be room for sociology of error – for explanations of why people get things wrong – but not for sociology of knowledge. Perhaps, though, the phrase 'sociology of knowledge' is shorthand for sociological investigation of the conditions in which knowledge is acquired. There is certainly room for study of such questions as why scientific discoveries and advances are made at the time and place they are. Are there hidden factors favouring or inhibiting such advances? But it is also true that human knowledge is affected or coloured by the social and cultural environment. So there is also room for sociological study of the manner in which knowledge is assimilated, expressed and communicated at different times. But of course in complicated areas such as religion it is naive to talk of knowledge and error as simple white or black alternatives. In all spheres outside the very simplest cases, knowledge-claims are bound to be incomplete and are highly likely to include some error or distortion. In these

---

* *Ideology and Utopia* (London: Routledge and Kegan Paul, 1936).
† London: Faber and Faber, 1969, and Harmondsworth: Penguin Books, 1973.

cases there is plenty of room for sociological (and psychological) study of the factors conditioning what passes for knowledge. The fact that the more complex the sphere of discourse the more we are driven to speak of knowledge-claims, or even of belief, rather than simply of knowledge, shows that we are aware of the at best partial and approximate nature of human apprehension in spheres such as religion. Perhaps it would have been better if sociologists right from the start had spoken of the sociology of belief.

We can see the need for sociological study of the factors conditioning religious belief (or unbelief) when we reflect on the wide variety of beliefs that are expressed and taught in the religion of the world. Even within a relatively restricted period in the history of a single religion such as Christianity, if one compares a typical nineteenth-century sermon on the nature of faith with a mid-twentieth-century sermon on the same topic, one finds the differences to be immense. Partly this will be due to conscious rethinking of the grounds and nature of faith by believers and theologians in the course of a hundred years; but partly, it is clear, the two preachers are unconsciously affected by their whole cultural and social environment in the way in which they speak. This fact was stressed in Chapter 1, where we were more interested in the continuities through the changes; but here we realise how much the sociologist can offer towards accounting for the differences.

The sociology of knowledge, then, investigates the inveterate tendency of the human mind to let unconscious factors shape or affect its responses to reality. These include highly distorting factors such as group interests and rationalisations of class attitudes. The more these can be brought into our awareness, the more we can guard against the distortions which they cause. Thus the theologian positively needs the critical work of the sociologist of knowledge.

There is, however, a somewhat self-defeating tendency to press the insights of the sociology of knowledge too far. I am not now thinking of the nineteenth-century theories of religious belief as fantasy or illusion which can themselves be regarded as the self-justifying rationalisations of atheism. I am thinking rather of the tendency in writers such as Berger to see all our ideas, concepts and beliefs as socially conditioned human constructs. On this view, we construct a whole system of beliefs – a 'life-world' – in which to feel at home; and our religious beliefs are those parts of the system which enable us to give ultimate meaning to our lives in spite of finitude and death. This view of human thinking is much too self-contained. Philosophers will argue about the theory of knowledge involved, but many will no doubt want to say that the way we represent the world to ourselves, however *conditioned* by social and cultural factors, is at least intended to conform to the realities over against us. In the light of our discussions of objectivity in Chapter 1, it will be clear that the theologian too will want to defend a realist theory of knowledge against the view that it is we who 'pour out meaning into reality'.*

Moreover, if theology adopts and maintains the critical methods urged in Chapter 1, it will be better placed to reject the charge of a religion's being, in the bad sense, an ideology. An ideology is a system of beliefs which has come to control people's thinking automatically and uncritically. The sociologist of knowledge will point out how different ideologies maintain themselves and contain built-in devices to enable them to cope with adverse criticism. Thus Marxists tend to reject criticism as itself a manifestation of bourgeois consciousness. Religion can operate in a similar way. This is not the way to remain open to the pressure of the realities with which we have

* *Ibid.* p. 36 (in the Penguin edition).

to do. Critical theology prevents religion from lapsing into an ideology.

The debate on secularisation, mentioned earlier, is a good example of the sociology of knowledge at work. Not only have institutions such as government, education and medicine gradually been freed from religious control, but the common attitudes of men and women to the world and to life have to a considerable extent become predominantly non-religious, at least in the west and in areas greatly affected by western culture and technology. The sociologist will try to pin-point the causal factors making for such widespread changes in attitude. He will investigate the effects of urbanisation, of rapid political and social change, of reliance on scientific method and so on. But he will also have to investigate reactions to secularisation, not least where it is enforced, as in communist countries. It is far from clear that religion is destined to disappear. The tendencies under investigation are, after all, only tendencies, and strong though the cultural and social pressures making for secularisation may be both in the western and the communist worlds, at the end of the day what will decide the question of the extent and limits of secularisation will be the ultimate realities with which men actually have to do.

Conclusion

Our brief examination of the sciences of man will have shown that there are many different ways of studying a particular human phenomenon. Provided we refrain from advancing an exhaustive theory on the basis of a single line of approach, we can recognise that the different methods are at once partial and complementary. Consider, for example, the Hebrew prophets. The psychologist of religion can make some suggestions about the type of personality revealed by the accounts which we have of Isaiah's or Ezekiel's visions. The sociologist,

The problems of theology

drawing on his comparative studies, can tell us something of the social function of the cultic prophets and something of the charismatic role of the canonical prophets in times of impending and actual disaster. The historian of ancient Israel will have something to say about the way in which a particular prophet, say, the second Isaiah, took over the inherited ideas of his religion and fashioned out of them a new vision which enabled Israel to survive the exile. The theologian will enquire into the revelatory significance of the prophetic faith for Israel's and our response to God.

Consider, secondly, a powerful religious symbol such as the fatherhood of God. The psychologist can tell us something of the origins of such a symbol in the childhood of the race, or in the collective unconscious of man. He will show, too, how a man's own childhood experiences will affect his ability to react to that symbol positively. The sociologist will compare religious traditions dominated by this symbolism with those which operate with different symbols, and trace the different consequences for their respective societies. The theologian is interested in what the believer makes of the symbolism which he has inherited and whether it can become for him a vehicle of faith.* Only if the sociology of knowledge is so all-embracing as to deprive us of the notions of truth, validity and knowledge, can it claim to have ruled out the theologian's talk of the God to whose reality religious symbols point.

---

* On religious symbols, see also below, pp. 144–9.

4

Theology and philosophy

The word 'philosophy' means love of wisdom, and it is man's passion for wisdom and understanding that has driven him to ask far-reaching questions about the ultimate nature of things and the basic forms of human knowledge. Ancient philosophy was to a large extent religious philosophy. In India, for example, the six traditional philosophical schools of Hinduism include complex analyses of man's nature, his ultimate identity with the all-pervading spirit, and techniques of achieving release into mystical awareness of this identity. Similarly, the theory and practice of Buddhism constitute a non-theistic religious philosophy – of more limited scope, since many ultimate questions were held by the Buddha to be unanswerable. In the west, philosophy began in ancient Greece as a form of speculation about cosmology, but soon developed, in the thought of Plato and Aristotle, into all-embracing views of man and the universe as dependent on a single transcendent source and goal, called by Plato 'the Good' or 'the One' and by Aristotle, more intelligibly, 'God'. This drive towards a philosophical monotheism led to the inclusion of theology in philosophy as one branch of metaphysics, which Aristotle defined as 'the science of being *qua* being'.

Christian theology, by contrast, in its first few centuries, when Christianity's distinctive doctrines were taking shape, was allegedly based on a particular divine self-revelation through the history of Israel and the life, death and resurrection of Jesus Christ. Nevertheless the early Fathers of the Church found the Greek philosophical tradition, especially Platonism, both necessary and

The problems of theology

useful for the systematic formulation of Christian doctrine. There was always something of a tension between the God of the Bible and the God of the philosophers, however. In later centuries it was Aristotle's philosophy that became the dominant theoretical tool in the working out of Christian theology, as indeed it had been for the early and medieval Arab theologians in the working out of Muslim philosophical theology. By the time of St. Thomas Aquinas (c. 1224–74), a clear picture of the relation between philosophy and theology had emerged, philosophy now being seen as preparing the ground for theology by proving the existence of God and some of his basic attributes, and providing the necessary concepts and distinctions for spelling out intelligibly God's further revelation of his nature and his relation to the world. Such a synthesis was possible through the dominance of the somewhat platonised Aristotelianism of the Middle Ages.

Since medieval times, however, philosophy has become increasingly fragmented. In the wake of the Renaissance and the rise of modern science, the very different philosophical approaches of rationalism and empiricism were developed, both suspicious of revelation-claims. The rationalists held that man's unaided reason was capable of arriving at the ultimate truth of things, while the empiricists appealed to the experience of the senses and tended towards scepticism where religion and theology were concerned. (There were, however, attempts in the eighteenth century to produce empiricist versions of Christian theology, themselves very hostile to the rationalist versions.) A notable turning point in the history of philosophy was the work of the German philosopher, Immanuel Kant (1724–1804), whose conviction that the only sure foundation for philosophical advance lay in the analysis of the necessary conditions of human experience led to increasing emphasis both in philosophy and theology on the theory of knowledge. Kant himself held that religion was a matter of moral policy and action, and that, while the reality of God could be postulated on the basis of an analysis of moral reason, theology as such was not a possibility for human theoretical reason.

Kant's successors in German idealism* were less sceptical, but their ambitious philosophical theories of absolute spirit tended to embrace religion and theology as only a stage towards absolute knowledge, in a manner comparable to certain strands of Indian religious philosophy. An attempt to mark out an independent basis for religion and theology in man's feeling of absolute dependence was made by Friedrich Schleiermacher (1768–1834).

The twentieth century has seen a strong reaction against metaphysics, and modern philosophy has become even more fragmented, the empiricist tradition receiving very rigid and strict reformulation in logical positivism, which rejected theology as meaningless. In Germany and France, existentialist philosophy, starting from a phenomenological analysis of lived human experience, sometimes found itself speaking of God, but more often became little more than the defence of human freedom in an alien world. Many Christian theologians, however, found in existentialism an ally in the articulation of their theology, just as in Martin Buber (1878–1965) Jewish philosophical theology took something of an existentialist form.

In reaction to logical positivism, a number of 'personalist' philosophies were developed, such as those of John MacMurray (1891–1976) and Michael Polanyi (1891–1976), the latter very interestingly superimposed upon an extremely impressive philosophy of science. In an older style, a school known as 'process philosophy', based on the thought of Alfred North Whitehead (1861–

---

* 'Idealism', in philosophy, means the view that mind or spirit is the ultimate reality.

The problems of theology

1947), has been adopted by several Christian theologians, especially in America, though their inclusion of God's reality within the scope of 'process' terminology has not met with very wide acceptance.

Most modern philosophy has become a much more technical and piecemeal affair. The dominant approach in Britain and America is now that of philosophical analysis, in which logical and analytic skills are applied to particular problems in the philosophy of mind, ethics and language. But a return to more metaphysical interests is shown in recent theories of meaning and truth and in the suggestion that our language, by its very structure, reveals the conception of reality with which we operate. There is a reluctance in professional philosophy today to suppose that it can extend this interest beyond the reality of the world around us as it discloses itself in human language (including that of science). The bearing of philosophical analysis on theology will be discussed below.

Evidently, the fragmented nature of philosophy since the Enlightenment makes it impossible to suppose that the theologian can expect any longer to have a stable philosophical base for the construction of a theological system. We shall see that, at best, the theologian can borrow only the general critical methods of analysis and perhaps a number of particular philosophical insights. He must stand on his own feet, as he tries to fashion what he has learned from experience, history and tradition into a coherent and comprehensive view. He must, of course, be ready to submit his theology to criticism by philosophers, just as he will wish to enter into critical discussion of their views.

Philosophical theories of religion

In our discussion of the phenomenology of religion and of the scientific study of religion, we noted the tendency

Theology and philosophy

for theories of religion surreptitiously to come to control the handling of the data. Such theories, whether negative or positive, are philosophical in nature. As we saw, phenomenology itself has no business to be offering theories of religion, and psychology, anthropology and sociology, strictly speaking, have the more limited aim of explaining *aspects* of religious belief and practice. As soon as a scientific theory such as Durkheim's or Freud's purports to explain the whole fact of religion, it becomes more than scientific, in that it goes beyond the strict evidence and interprets it according to a particular philosophical position.

Empiricist philosophers have been inclined to adopt such negative theories. The Scottish philosopher, David Hume (1711–76), in his *A Natural History of Religion*, offered a crude theory of the origin and nature of religion in terms of man's fear and credulity. The logical positivists, as already mentioned, rejected religious and theological statements as meaningless, in accordance with their over-strict verificationist criterion of meaning, whereby only such statements as can be verified by appeal to the senses are allowed to count as statements of fact. The attempt of R. B. Braithwaite, from within the empiricist school, to rescue religious language as simply portraying, in story form, a set of ethical commitments, is a more positive approach and constitutes the classical example of a 'non-cognitivist' analysis of religious belief. (A 'non-cognitivist' analysis is one which purportedly shows that no factual knowledge-claim is really being made at all.)

Much more positive philosophical theories of religion in general are to be found in German idealism. By far the most important of these is that of Georg Wilhelm Friedrich Hegel (1770–1831). While Hegel was critical, in his early writings, of what he called 'positive' religion – that is, religion authoritatively taught on the basis of a particular historical tradition – he nevertheless espoused a creative religion of love and spirit, such as he conceived Christianity originally to have been. In his mature system, he saw religion as an essential element in the awakening of the human mind to consciousness of absolute truth, and Christianity as the absolute religion, in that it expressed most clearly the unity of finite and infinite in its doctrine of the incarnation. However, Hegel's philosophical system carried him beyond theism in that he came to see the history of philosophy as the history of the self-unfolding of absolute spirit, thus blurring the creator–creature distinction and moving in the direction of pantheism. His concept of incarnation as a principle of the unity of finite and infinite rather than a particular historical event reinforces this tendency; and his view that religion represents pictorially what philosophy must ultimately grasp in terms of the 'Concept' shows that, for Hegel, philosophy takes priority over religion and gives it a subordinate place in the development of spirit.

Mention has been made of Schleiermacher's attempt to find an independent basis for religion and theology in the religious consciousness of man. Another philosophical theory of religion of a similar kind is to be found in Rudolf Otto's *The Idea of the Holy*, mentioned in Chapter 2 as an example of the way in which an allegedly phenomenological study can turn into a philosophy of religion. Otto held that the 'numinous' experience of the 'holy', characteristic of religion the world over, was an *a priori*, underived factor in the human spirit. He held, further, that the non-rational and rational aspects of the 'holy', were united most lucidly in Christianity. Our suspicion now arises, however, that Otto's philosophical theory of religion is being made subservient to a Christian theological theory of religion.

These examples might lead us to wonder whether philosophy really possesses the vantage point from which to reach an adequate theory of religion. Once again we can put the matter hypothetically. If God does not exist, then we would expect it to be at least possible for philosophy to give a complete and adequate account of the phenomenon of religion, whether as meaningless, as illusory, as a symbolic representation of society, as a disguised form of ethics, or as a pictorial anticipation of man's consciousness of absolute truth. If, however, God does exist, the question of philosophy's ability to grasp divine truth becomes much more uncertain. It may be that human wisdom is capable of so reading religious experience the world over as to develop an adequate theory of religion. This is the view of those who speak of the 'perennial philosophy' – a theory of mysticism as the essence of religion, manifested in different forms at all times and places. Alternatively it might be held, on philosophical grounds, that the divine reality is manifested gradually in the evolution of religion from its earliest beginnings to its fullest flowering in, say, Christianity. But how far is this really a philosophical judgement? It does not look like an independent philosophical assessment of the history of religions. It looks much more like a theory developed on the basis of a particular religion's own self-understanding, that is, a theological theory of religion.

Such a philosophico-theological theory of religion is actually most plausible in the context of a religion which does not rely on the idea of a special revelation. As we shall see in the next section and in the next chapter, it is most at home in Indian religion rather than in the 'religions of a book' – Judaism, Christianity and Islam. Within these religions it is much more common to find a clear demarcation between metaphysics and theology, between what human reason alone can discover about God and what is disclosed solely through revelation by God himself.

Metaphysics and theology

In this section we shall look briefly at a number of classical treatments in the different religions of the relation between philosophy and theology.

A good example of the Indian tendency not to make strict lines of demarcation between the two is to be found in the writings of Rāmānuja (eleventh century AD). Probably the best known of the six schools of Hindu philosophy is that of the Vedānta, claiming to spell out the inner meaning of the ancient Hindu scriptures. Its more familiar form is the non-dualist (Advaita) Vedānta of Shankara (*c.* 788–*c.* 820 AD). This can hardly be called a philosophical *theology*, since its fundamental teaching is that of the identity of the soul with the all-pervading spirit (Brahman), conceived of ultimately in impersonal terms. Rāmānuja advanced against this a modified form of Advaita Vedānta, in which the ultimately personal qualities of God are affirmed, and it is taught that the self finds salvation or release in personal union with the divine. For Rāmānuja there is an analogy between the self and its body on the one hand and God and the world on the other. The points of similarity and of difference in this analogy are carefully worked out by Rāmānuja in respect of such fundamental topics as the reality of the world, its source in God, and the destiny of souls in relation to God. It is at once a philosophy and a theology, an attempt to make sense both of Rāmānuja's own devotional religious experience and of the philosophical tradition which he inherited. But it is important to realise that the Hindu scriptures which that tradition interprets are themselves philosophico-religious treatises expressing insights which each teacher can help his pupil to experience for himself.

The medieval Persian philosopher, known in the west as Avicenna (980–1037), makes an interesting comparison. Avicenna was a Muslim doctor, self-taught in philosophy, and very much influenced by Aristotelianism and Neoplatonism. His notion of God as the one necessary source of all existing things, himself absolute truth,

goodness, life and love, owes as much to these philosophical traditions as to the revealed scripture of Islam,
the Qu'ran, and indeed his view of the world as eternally
emanating from the divine intelligence and of God as
necessarily creator of the world is in apparent conflict
with the teachings of the Qu'ran. We notice at once how
much more difficult it is for the Muslim philosopher to
accommodate alleged revelation than for Rāmānuja.
For the Hindu, philosophical and religious insight *are*
revelation. Nonetheless we find in Avicenna a philosophical justification of revelation, at least in the sense of
the communication through prophets of the law of
human life. This is held to be necessitated by the divine
goodness. Avicenna goes on to discuss the possibility of
growth in mystical awareness of the divine truth, indicating thereby the influence on him of the 'Sufi' tradition of
Islamic mysticism. The tension between metaphysics and
theology in Avicenna, and the tendency for metaphysics
to prevail, are explained by the fact that for Muslims
generally revelation is primarily revelation of God's *will*
for man rather than of God's nature.

The Muslim philosophers have an important place in
medieval Islam. Judaism, by contrast, has seldom
fostered philosophical, or indeed theological speculation. The figure of Moses Maimonides (1135–1204) is a
somewhat exceptional one. Maimonides wrote his
Guide of the Perplexed to help those well-versed in the
religious tradition of Judaism who were nevertheless
puzzled by the apparent clashes between religion and
philosophy. Maimonides is much less positive than Avicenna in his view of what philosophy can tell us about
God. For Maimonides philosophy removes false conceptions of God through its insistence on what God is
not. Maimonides' chief concern, however, is with God's
ordering of creation; for, unlike Avicenna and in conson-
ance with his own tradition, he rejects the notion of the
eternity of the world. Nevertheless he does not set revela-

tion over against philosophy, since he regards the prophets, through whom God's revelation comes, as themselves men of acute philosophical intellect, even though their main concern is with moral and political education. In this respect he has more in common with Avicenna, and indeed the Muslim emphasis on the revealed will of God for men is comparable with and no doubt influenced by that of the older Jewish tradition.

It is an interesting indication of the possibility of a common natural theology, at least between Judaism, Christianity and Islam, that the medieval Christian theologians were much influenced by the Jewish and Muslim philosophers. This was largely owing to the common influence of Aristotle (and of Neoplatonism). Indeed it was the Muslim philosophers who were instrumental in the transmission of knowledge of Aristotle's works to the west. But the Christian philosophers of the Middle Ages, of whom the greatest was St. Thomas Aquinas, made a much more sustained effort to reconcile the knowledge of God yielded by philosophy with that yielded by revelation. This reconciliation was an important enterprise for Aquinas both because he believed that philosophy could give some knowledge of God and of his relation to the world, and because, on his view, revelation gave much more than knowledge of the *will* of God. He insisted that revealed knowledge of God as the Blessed Trinity went beyond the reach of philosophical thought, but he was at pains to show that it did not contradict the notion of God's unity and simplicity which philosophical reflection could advance. An interesting example of the relation between metaphysics and theology in Aquinas is his view that philosophy could not prove that the world had a temporal beginning. This we learn from revelation. But this is not a typical example, since revelation is not usually called upon so much to settle undecided questions in metaphysics as to supplement and make more precise the knowledge which philosophy actually achieves. Moreover for the common man, revelation includes those truths which philosophy could teach him were he philosophically minded. The possibility of positive knowledge of God, whether coming from philosophy or revelation, is defended by Aquinas through his highly influential doctrine of analogy. It is because there is an 'analogy of being' between the world and God, and especially between man, made in the image of God, and God, that we can use the language of human perfections in speaking, admittedly in a more exalted sense, of God's perfection. Aquinas is well aware that, so far as our grasp of the meaning of words like 'love', 'will', 'intellect' and 'goodness' is concerned, we learn it from their ordinary human use first of all, and then extend it, by analogy, to the case of God. Yet, so far as reality itself is concerned, it is God who possesses these attributes supremely, and our love, will, intellect and goodness are but a pale shadow of his.

Something will be said at the end of this chapter about Aquinas's philosophical arguments for the existence of God. For the present, we simply note the way in which a common philosophical tradition enabled the medieval philosophers of Judaism, Christianity and Islam to advance, if not identical, at least comparable views of God and his relation to the world. We can also see that their differences largely stem from the influence of their own particular religious traditions on their philosophical thinking.

For purposes of comparison and contrast, I select one modern Christian philosophical theologian, Paul Tillich, whose views on the being of God were mentioned in Chapter 1. From what has been said already about the fragmentation of philosophy since the Renaissance, we shall expect a very different and much more controversial picture of the relation between metaphysics and theology to emerge. In fact the philosophical views which Tillich adopts as the basis of his approach are hardly typical of the twentieth century. There is no such common ground today. Tillich combines an old-fashioned reliance on German idealism, especially that of Friedrich Wilhelm Joseph von Schelling (1775–1854), with a particular brand of existentialism. The former lies behind Tillich's use of the notions of 'Being Itself' and 'the Ground of Being' to characterise the ultimate reality with which religion and theology are dealing, and the latter – existentialism – lies behind Tillich's talk of 'ultimate concern'. It also influences his well-known method of 'correlation', whereby theology's answers are held to meet questions forced upon us by philosophical – in this case, existentialist – assessment of the human predicament. We note that the more modern philosophical influence – existentialism – is much more concerned with the human side, with the situation in which man finds himself and with the way religion meets that need, than with the object of theology, God. In order to speak philosophically of God, Tillich goes back to an older, and to many moderns discredited, type of philosophy. Nonetheless it is interesting that Tillich makes this attempt to hold metaphysics and theology together. This applies also to his notion of revelation. In Tillich's writings, the specifically Christian element, the power of 'new being' made possible by the 'coming of Jesus as the Christ', is discussed in philosophical terms, rather than in the purely theological language of 'the Word of God' characteristic of the dominant strand in twentieth-century Christian theology.

Of the five thinkers mentioned in this section, only Rāmānuja and Tillich can be said to have a genuinely comprehensive theology of the different religions of the world. We have noted the common natural theology of the medievals, but their different views on the source of revelation – the Hebrew Bible, the Qu'ran, the New Testament – introduce restricted 'horizons of meaning' at the point where metaphysics gives way to revelation.

Theology and philosophy

The Indian tradition, by contrast, especially the Bhagavad Gītā, with Krishna's famous saying, 'even those
who lovingly devote themselves to other gods and sacrifice to them, full filled with faith, do really worship Me
though the rite may differ from the norm', enables
Rāmānuja to embrace the whole religious life of man
within his system.* Paul Tillich, too, increasingly came
to devote his attention to the problem of other religions,
and, interestingly enough, at the end of his life, remarked
that, if he were to rewrite his *Systematic Theology*, he
would make the history of religions rather than philosophy the basis of his theological answer to the questions
raised by the existentialist analysis of the human predicament. Tillich's theory of the symbolism of the different
religions, through which it is possible to break in order to
find the living heart of all religions, is at least a contribution to discussion of this central problem of theology.†
We shall see reason to doubt its adequacy, but the theologian can hardly return to the medieval position.

Theology and philosophical analysis

The less ambitious and more piecemeal approaches of
modern British and American philosophy are reflected in
the rarity of systems such as Tillich's and the preference
for attention to particular problems and to the analysis
of particular concepts found in the religious traditions of
the world. Much of this work is done at a level of gener-
ality which makes it applicable to most of the theistic religions. We can illustrate this work under three headings:
discussion of the great philosophers and their views on
religion, discussion of problems in the theory of religious
knowledge, and discussion of particular problem areas
in theistic views of the world.

* The Bhagavad Gītā, trans. R. C. Zaehner (London: OUP, 1969),
9.23.
† On these problems, see, further, pp. 144–8, below.

The problems of theology

Although few today would call themselves, without further ado, Platonists, Aristotelians, Leibnizians, Humeans or Kantians, the fact remains that Plato, Aristotle, Leibniz, Hume and Kant, and other great philosophers of the past, had important things to say about religion and theology. Their views are well worth scrutiny today. Some of the points they made retain validity and need to be reckoned with by the modern theologian. Even where they went wrong, their views have sometimes been so influential that they require detailed study and refutation before the theologian can proceed in a way that his philosophical colleagues can respect, let alone accept. Consequently the philosophy of religion is frequently begun in an academic context by means of an examination of Plato's and Aristotle's metaphysics. We investigate the degree to which Plato's work renders the very enterprise of metaphysics an intelligible one, and the degree to which Aristotle's arguments for the existence of an 'unmoved mover' can be used in the case for theism today. We examine Leibniz's solution of the problem of evil, and Hume's rejection of the design argument for the existence of God as well as his criticism of belief in miracles. Kant's systematic restriction of the conditions of human experience to the sphere of sense, structured by the knowing mind, has, as has been said, proved a great stumbling block to all subsequent attempts to do theology, and the philosopher of religion will need to examine the ways in which theologians today either reject Kant's framework, or expand it to include the reality of God among the conditions of experience. Clearly it will make a great difference to theology whether one can reject Kant and speak objectively of God, or whether one must adopt a Kantian approach and expand it in order to speak indirectly of God as presupposed in all intelligible discourse. A great deal of careful analysis is carried out in such examinations of the great philosophers.

Mention of Kant will have shown that among the

problems to be analysed those relating to the theory of knowledge are particularly important. Study of the problem of the possibility of religious knowledge will involve fresh examination of the arguments for the existence of God and analysis of religious language and the nature of religious faith. The twentieth-century recognition of the importance of language, both as the medium of communication and as revelatory of an implicit metaphysics, means that philosophers of religion today will need to pay close attention to religious language – that is, to ordinary language as used in religious contexts – both for its points in common with and for its differences from linguistic usage in other contexts. Very different views are possible here. Mention has been made of R. B. Braithwaite's attempt to treat religious language as ethical language, buttressed by a set of stories with no factual content. Another approach is that of several philosophers, including D. Z. Phillips, influenced by the later philosophy of Wittgenstein, who see the language of faith and worship in a given religious tradition as a relatively autonomous affair, creating a sphere of life and discourse which can have and need have no defence on grounds common to believer and unbeliever. This approach, rather like that of the phenomenology of religion, often succeeds very well in bringing out the inner meaning, to those taking part, of religious language, attitudes and rites, but fails to do justice, philosophically, to the explicit or implicit belief of religious believers that they are responding to something that is ultimately the case. When believers speak of the reality of God, they do not use the word 'reality' in a totally different sense from the reality of things and persons but rather in an analogous sense. A proper philosophical critique should reckon with that fact and subject it either to attack or to defence.*

* See P. Sherry, *Religion, Truth and Language Games* (London: Macmillan, 1977).

75

The problems of theology

The influence of Wittgenstein on the philosophy of religion is not restricted to such 'non-cognitivist' analyses of religious language. In the writings of the logician, Peter Geach, we find an exploration of theistic concepts such as omnipotence, omniscience and providence, which owe a great deal to the tradition of philosophical logic in which the names of Frege and Wittgenstein stand out.* This brings us to the third area of the philosopher of religion's interest, namely, discussion of particular problems in theism. A concept in the same range as those just mentioned is that of God's necessary existence. Many philosophers, following Hume and Kant, have held that only statements and propositions can be necessary, and that to speak of necessary existence is a confusion. But it has become clear that to speak of God's necessary existence is not to commit oneself to the 'ontological argument', whereby God's existence is supposed to be proved simply by analysis of the concept of God. On the contrary God's necessary existence is shown by the fact that, if he exists, he cannot simply happen to exist or to have come into existence or be capable of going out of existence. He is, in Anselm's phrase, 'without beginning or end or composition of parts', and of such an infinite and absolute nature as not to give rise to calls for further explanation of his being in being. This is sometimes called 'factual' or 'ontological' necessity by way of contrast with the 'logical' necessity of propositions.† On the other hand man's discovery that this is what God is like takes time. The history of religion does not begin with such a concept of God. Consequently it is only at a certain stage that the concept of God acquires these connotations and it becomes part of the

---

* *God and the Soul*, (London: Routledge and Kegan Paul, 1969), and *Providence and Evil* (Cambridge University Press, 1977).
† See J. Hick, *Arguments for the Existence of God* (London: Macmillan, 1970), chs. 5 and 6.

definition of God that, if he exists, then he exists necessarily. Once this inclusion of factual necessity in the concept of God has been achieved, however, certain logical consequences inevitably follow – as from any definition; but such logical truths about God are not to be confused with the ontological argument. They are logical consequences of a concept of God that has gradually established itself as a result of metaphysical thinking and the exigencies of religious worship. Clarity in the handling of notions such as 'necessity' in religious discourse is an important skill to be acquired by the philosopher of religion.

Other problems in this third area include the analysis of the concepts of time and eternity, the relation between omniscience and human freedom, the age old problem of evil, and the sense of and case for belief in life after death. There is not space to discuss these problems here, but they are all examples of the areas in which dialogue between philosopher and theologian in a thoroughly rational and critical spirit must take place.

Philosophical theology today

In the last section the phrase 'philosophy of religion' was used, and its piecemeal, analytic character illustrated. In turning now to speak of 'philosophical theology', we should pause to reflect on the difference between these two expressions. The philosopher of religion is someone who, on the basis of his training in philosophy, turns his attention to religion and theology and their problems. We have seen how the nature of this enterprise has changed. Hitherto the philosopher approached religion from the standpoint of his own system of thought about the world. He either fitted religion into that system or marked out further territory where he himself could not proceed and handed it over to the theologian with his revelation-tradition. Nowadays the philosopher may well have no particular system, but rather a set of logical and analytical techniques which he proceeds to apply to the concepts of religion and theology. The philosophical theologian, by contrast, is first and foremost a theologian. We have seen how, as such, he inevitably finds himself, at least to start with, operating on the basis of a particular religious tradition and its revelation-claims. He simply uses philosophy to help him articulate the sense and structure of that tradition. Of course his way of doing this has changed, as philosophy has changed. No longer does he adapt a particular philosophical system to his theological use, as the medievals did. Where he does still do this, as is the case with process theology, based on the philosophy of A. N. Whitehead, it seldom carries conviction except with devotees. The theologian is much more likely these days simply to use the same logical and analytical techniques upon his theological material as does his colleague in the philosophy faculty. This means that, despite the differences just mentioned, philosophy of religion and philosophical theology are much closer together than hitherto. Only if the theologian tries to preserve a private or restricted source of information can he maintain the older demarcation between philosophy and theology. Provided he adopts a critical attitude and, in Pannenberg's words already quoted, lets 'theology be discussed without reservations in the context of critical rationality', the only difference between philosopher and theologian will be that the latter makes ultimate reality and the God allegedly revealed in the religions explicitly the object of his interest. He does not seek to preserve that revelation from philosophical scrutiny.

Our discussion of the demarcation between philosophy and theology implies some criticism of the narrower approaches of modern philosophy. Valuable as the logical and analytic methods of contemporary philosophy undoubtedly are, the theologian is bound to feel that the collapse of the great philosophical systems of the past has made the modern philosopher over-timorous regarding the questions of total meaning and ultimate reality. He may also feel that philosophers, both in the past when constructing systems and in the present when rejecting them, have tended to pay insufficient attention to the religions and their revelation-claims. There is this to be said for the work of A. N. Whitehead, that he attempted to reconstruct a philosophical system, in the awareness both of modern logical techniques and of the data of religion, even if that system itself tends to distort the religious data in embracing them. On the other hand, it is not surprising that modern philosophy has more usually ignored religion and theology, given the latter's largely pre-critical nature even in recent times.

If, however, theology becomes open and critical in the way defended in Chapter 1, it will be apparent that the old distinction between natural and revealed theology, between what reason can achieve and what requires revelation, breaks down. As will be shown in the next chapter, reason and revelation cannot be treated as different sources of knowledge. On the contrary revelation-claims, despite being channelled through particular historical traditions, are part of the data upon which reason has to operate. The fact that the philosopher pays less attention to the religious data than does the theologian is just unfortunate. It can no longer be a matter of principle.

On the other hand, the difficulty remains that unlike the modern philosopher, each theologian still works within a given historical tradition, such as that of Hinduism or Christianity. It is easy to reply that in fact the modern philosopher also works within a culturally relative context (as a comparison of Indian and British philosophy shows). But the theological 'tribalism' is more blatant and apparently more unavoidable, given the nature of religion as it has developed in the different

The problems of theology

streams of human history. At this point we revert to the need for comparative theology. The parochial nature of theology can be overcome only if philosophical theology is undertaken on a comparative basis.

The case for theism

If we are right in supposing that in modern theology reason is to be exercised on all the data, including revelation-claims, then what Basil Mitchell has called the 'cumulative case' for theism* will include not only the old general arguments for the existence of God, but also specific arguments based on the actual history of religions.

We conclude this chapter by sketching the kind of cumulative case for theism which the philosophical theologian might put forward for consideration and criticism.

He might begin as follows: the fact that anything exists at all is a great mystery. This is the starting point for metaphysical reflection into the possibility of some ultimate explanation for the fact that the world exists. But the *cosmological* argument which postulates a necessary and self-sufficient cause or ground for the existence of the world does not rest on the bare fact of the existence of something rather than nothing. It proceeds rather from the fact that the world apparently consists of finite, perishable things, which do not, so far as we can see, contain within themselves an explanation for their being in being. Admittedly when we press back from the structured perishable world of living things, material objects, planets, suns and galaxies, to the basic stuff of the universe, that is, to the fundamental particles and forces of

* *The Justification of Religious Belief* (London: Macmillan, 1973).

which the universe is composed, we reach a level of imperishable, though still finite reality. This basic stuff or energy still does not contain within itself an explanation for its being in being, though, given the basic material, what has emerged from it in the course of cosmic evolution can probably be explained. Now what strikes us, as we contemplate the basic stuff of the universe, with its astonishing potential for change, combination and development in the direction of ever higher complexity, is its inherently rational structure. Moreover out of the process of cosmic evolution, there has emerged, at least in this corner of this galaxy, and quite possibly elsewhere (though we do not *know* this), a world of life, consciousness and intelligence. The rationality of the universe and the fact that out of it have emerged rational beings constitute the grounds for the argument for *design* (the *teleological* argument). In a post-Darwinian age, this does not take the form of appeals to particular phenomena irrespective of their history and context, but rather to the whole process from the clouds of inter-stellar dust to the emergence of intelligent life on this planet. The steps in the process are partly (and, one hopes, increasingly) understood, but the fact that fundamental particles have it in them to combine in this way demands a more ultimate explanation than science can ever be expected to give. Nor does the fact that *we* are rational beings suffice to explain *our* preference for explanations in terms of intelligent design. The argument rather, is that our rationality and that of the universe's structure *can only* be explained in terms of intelligent design. To prefer to say that that is just how things are is not to prefer an equally rational alternative; it is to prefer no account at all.

The cumulative case now proceeds to investigate the human world further. Certainly some explanation of the nature and extent of the world's suffering and evil is called for if our design argument is to be sustained, but equally the fact of human goodness and the high values which human beings can come to perceive and to prefer, require to be accounted for, if our world-view is to satisfy our minds. This is the starting point of the *moral* argument for theism, though it can be expanded to include aesthetic values too. (We can call it, broadly, the *axiological* argument.) Of course it is disputed whether all this is just subjective preference, but a surprising number of philosophers themselves, on close analysis of ethics and aesthetics, are simply not persuaded by such subjectivist views. Both the objectivity of moral and aesthetic values and their precarious hold in the world as we know it are best explained in terms of an absolute and transcendent source of all value, which may most naturally be equated with the transcendent source of the world's being.

The reality of the transcendent is suggested not only by these cosmological, teleological and axiological arguments. A general anthropology, such as is attempted in Pannenberg's *What is Man?** or in Don Cupitt's *The Leap of Reason*,† by concentrating on man's openness for the future, his freedom and his self-transcendence, can contribute to the case for a wider horizon of meaning and intelligibility than is given in the purely scientific study of the world. Even the sociologist, Peter Berger, in his *A Rumour of Angels*,‡ has listed 'signals of transcendence' such as play, humour, hope, man's propensity for order and his moral sense of outrage, all pointing beyond the limited scope of sociological explanation.

Next the cumulative case might include reference to the fact of religion in human society the world over. The

* English trans., Philadelphia: Fortress Press, 1970.
† London: Sheldon Press, 1976.
‡ Garden City, New York: Doubleday, 1969, and Harmondsworth: Allen Lane, Penguin Press, 1970, and Pelican Books, 1971.

factors which led Otto to speak of the 'religious *a priori*'* need to be accounted for. Note that, at this stage, the emphasis is on the widespread fact of religious experience. It is a mistake, in constructing a public cumulative case for theism, to put too much weight on one's own private inner experience. On the other hand the fact that people, perhaps including oneself, can become existentially convinced of the reality of God, will contribute to the case for theism.

The public case continues with a scrutiny of the history of the religions for their capacity to develop all-embracing world-views that at once do justice to all other knowledge, and also provide convincing evidence to support their revelation-claims. This is the point at which appeal to revelation can become part of a philosophical argument. For it is no longer an appeal to an unquestionable authority, but rather to the inner rationality of an alleged revelation. It is argued, in other words, that this revelation, if true, would make greater sense of the world and of life than would any other world-view. Something was said above, in Chapter 2, about criteria of preference among such total religious world-views.

St. Thomas Aquinas has been much criticised for ending each of his five proofs of the existence of God with the words 'and this is what everybody understands by God'. It has been felt that this represents too easy an identification of the God of philosophy with the God of religion. But in fact it *is* easy to identify the source of all being and value with the one whom the religions hold to be revealed in their respective traditions. And the more we allow revelation-claims to be subjected to the scrutiny of critical reason, the less we will be inclined to see an unbridgeable gap here.

The kind of cumulative case sketched in this section is

---

* R. Otto, *The Idea of the Holy*, English trans. (London: OUP, 1923, and Harmondsworth: Penguin Books, 1959), chs. 12 and 15.

not a deductive proof – that is, the derivation of logical consequences from agreed premises. Nor is it an inductive proof – a general conclusion reached from a large number of similar instances. It is rather an example of the kind of reasoning which John Henry Newman called 'illation',* in which a whole number of different threads are drawn together and seen to point in a certain direction. The philosopher, Anthony Flew, pooh-poohs this kind of argument, on the grounds that ten leaky buckets hold no more water than one leaky bucket. That analogy is quite inappropriate. It depends on treating each element in the cumulative case as a failed deductive or inductive proof. That is totally to miss the point of the kind of informal reasoning commonly used by archaeologists, historians, jurists, politicians and literary critics, as well as by theologians, in assessing the joint significance of a whole range of relevant factors. It is rather a question of the critical mind's ability to find an intelligible pattern in all the evidence taken together. We judge that these factors point in the direction of theism, and then, perhaps, our experience is found to confirm that judgement.

---

* *A Grammar of Assent* (London: Burns, Oates, 1870), ch. 9.

5

The problem of revelation

Revelation and rationality

Western philosophers have been extremely suspicious of the notion of revelation. This is because, traditionally, divine revelation was held, particularly by Jews, Christians and Muslims, to consist in the authoritative declaration of certain fundamental truths and injunctions, inaccessible to man's unaided powers of reason and reflection. Philosophers, by contrast, have tried to make sense of the world and human life in ways accessible, at least in principle, to any reflective mind. The apparent irrationality of revelation-claims is that they allegedly rest on an unchallengeable and untestable basis. Moreover, as soon as serious attention is paid to the fact of rival revelation-claims in the different religions, it appears that the authority of any one religion's revelation-claims is undermined, or at least put in question.

However, this is not the only conception of divine revelation to be found in the history of religions. The Indian writer, K. Satchidananda Murty, in his book *Revelation and Reason in Advaita Vedānta,** asserts that all knowledge is revelation, since reality discloses itself to us as we discover and penetrate its nature. All discovery and experience of God are God's disclosure of himself to us. Murty illustrates this view quite liberally by quotations from the whole history of religions, east and west. On this view divine revelation is not inaccessible to the enquiring spirit. On the contrary, as any man

* London: OUP, 1956.

learns or trains himself to experience the world religiously, revelation occurs.

Even the religions of Semitic origin, with their great emphasis on a holy book, containing the special revelation of God, also, as we saw in the last chapter, for the most part teach that *some* knowledge of God is universally accessible to human reason or experience. Their theologians call this general revelation, by contrast with special revelation to prophets and apostles enshrined in a book. In so far as this knowledge is thought to be theoretical knowledge, general revelation is the result of 'natural theology' — knowledge of God acquired through rational reflection. In so far as it is more a question of experiential knowledge, it is either mystical experience or the sense of the numinous that is held to mediate knowledge of God, wherever such forms of religious consciousness are found. But for religions such as Judaism, Christianity and Islam, this general knowledge and experience of God are not enough. The nature and especially the will of God are held to be further specified through particular communications from the divine to certain chosen messengers. The eventual result of such revelation is 'holy scripture'.

What should our attitude be to this problem of revelation and rationality? Clearly we cannot dictate in advance what there is for human reason to work on. Reason does not create the objects which we think about. Certainly we invent or propose *theories* to account for our experience of the world, but we test these theories against the facts. It is reality that has the last word. We can accept no arbitrary restriction on what there is to think about. We are bound to try to reflect rationally on whatever comes to us through our experience of life in the world and through the world's history. There is, of course, the question of the limits of our rational powers and so, correlatively, of the sort of objects that can come within their purview. We are finite limited beings and there is no reason to suppose that our rational powers are adequate to anything and everything that there is.

But the limited scope of our rational powers has been greatly exaggerated. It is very far from clear that we are limited solely to the field of our sense experience and to the formal categories of thought. Our awareness may begin with what comes to us through the senses, but our ability to organise these materials in ways which yield knowledge of much more than physical objects is quite clear. We have only to think of our knowledge of other people and of ourselves. These too can become objects of rational reflection. So can the aesthetic and ethical values which we perceive in the world about us and in human life and action. The claim of the religions is that just as all these things reveal themselves to us in our experience and reflection, so too does God reveal his nature and will in and through the religious traditions of man and the experiences which they make possible. We have no business to rule out *a priori* the possibility that among the objects given to our experience and rational reflection are the reality, nature and will of God.

How these things are given to us is, of course, in dispute. Is it just through rational reflection, mystical experience and the sense of the numinous? Or is it also through prophets and holy books, through historical events and through the developing traditions of faith? The suggestion that is being put forward here is that both sets of possibilities can be explored and thought about rationally. It is not only the religious experiences on which Indian religion concentrates, nor just that area of alleged knowledge of God which comes under the traditional heading of natural theology that can be investigated and tested by any sympathetic open mind. The revelation-claims centred on prophets and holy books, and the doctrinal systems that have been built up on them, can also themselves be subjected to rational scrutiny for their success in making comprehensive sense, intellectually and religiously, of all the data that come to us through experience *and* history.

There is a sense in which, if this approach is possible, the distinction between natural and revealed theology breaks down. Sacred scriptures are no longer to be thought of as unquestionable authorities. There is no irreconcilable opposition between reason and revelation. We are to use all our faculties of critical scrutiny upon all the alleged data including the revelation-claims of the different religions and their traditions of faith. Whether the 'religions of a book' have the flexibility to adopt this approach is one of the main problems of theology today.

In another sense a fundamental difference remains between those religions which teach that knowledge of God is a universal possibility irrespective of special acts of God in history, and those religions which teach that we are to look to history for further revelation. Both claims may be open to rational scrutiny, but they are very different claims, as we shall see.

Sacred scriptures

Not all sacred scriptures have the same form nor the same kind of claimed authority. The scriptures of Hinduism, the Vedas and more especially the Upanishads, express the insights and teachings of the ancient sages of India, who discovered the way of mystical and philosophical penetration into the world of the spirit. These scriptures are called 'revelation' but they are not usually thought of as communications from the divine, but rather as records of spiritual discovery which the disciple can come to experience for himself through meditative techniques, learned from the master. The Bhagavad Gītā, the Song of the Lord, has much more in common with scriptures from the other religions of personal theism. It puts its teaching in the form of discourses by

The problem of revelation

the divine Krishna, the Avatār of Vishnu, and includes at its climax an awesome theophany of Vishnu, a vision comparable to those of Isaiah or Ezekiel in the Hebrew Bible. Nevertheless the burden of its teaching, like that of the Upanishads, is to commend an experiential way of finding spiritual release, though here the emphasis is on the way of devotion to the god.

More comparable to the Upanishads are the scriptures of ancient Chinese religion, especially Taoism. The Tao Te Ching consists in a long poem setting out the principles of this particular form of philosophical mysticism. The Analects of Confucius, by contrast, consist chiefly of ethical and social teaching, though in a cosmic setting.

To turn to the so-called 'religions of a book', we find a great contrast between the Hebrew Bible and the Christian New Testament on the one hand and the Qu'ran on the other. The Hebrew Bible consists of many different kinds of writing – sagas, histories, legal texts, prophetic books, wisdom writings – from many different hands over many hundreds of years, and the New Testament too, though dating from a much briefer period, is a very diverse collection of gospels, narratives, letters and visionary writings; whereas the Qu'ran allegedly consists of the revelations of God to a single mind, the last and greatest of the prophets, Muhammad. Nevertheless, despite these differences, the status of these scriptures in Judaism, Christianity and Islam looks at first sight very similar. For Jews the Hebrew Bible, for Christians the New Testament as well as the Old, for Muslims the Qu'ran constitutes the Word of God, the human authors or author being thought of as instrumental in the process of divine revelation to mankind. The 'holy book' for these religions, throughout most of their history, constitutes both the source and the norm of special divine revelation over and above whatever general revelation may be admitted in these religions. Such an attitude to sacred scriptures can easily lead to a position known as 'fundamentalism',* namely, the view that the scripture in question is divinely inspired, free from error, and uniquely and solely authoritative for faith and morals. Fundamentalism is a fairly extreme position in that it tends to treat the scriptures in their literal sense as unquestionable and divinely guaranteed. It is perfectly possible, and perhaps more common, to regard the scriptures not so much as *being*, but rather as *containing* divine revelation, so that some interpretation is required before the real meaning of the scriptures or of the reality to which they point, can emerge. But even such non-fundamentalist attitudes to sacred scriptures still involve treating the scriptures of one's own tradition as uniquely authoritative and ignoring the others.

Fundamentalism is not refuted by the fact that different people in different religions take up fundamentalist attitudes to different scriptures, but the fact that any religious group can make this move – that, for example, the Book of Mormon is so regarded by members of the Church of Jesus Christ of the Latter-Day Saints – renders fundamentalism an extremely precarious and implausible position, and largely contributes to the disrepute in which the very notion of revelation stands in the eyes of philosophers. Even non-fundamentalist attitudes to scripture, for example the biblicism of many non-fundamentalist Christians who accept that the Bible requires a good deal of interpretation, but who still regard it as uniquely inspired and authoritative and continue to ignore the scriptures of other religions, are to some extent tarred with the same brush. Only if the actual content of the scriptures in question can be shown to have a revelatory power greater than that of any other, can the claim of that scripture to yield special knowledge of God really be justified and sustained.

* See J. Barr, *Fundamentalism* (London: SCM Press, 1977).

The problem of revelation

This means that at least the *formal* contrast between the scriptures of Indian religion, consisting in the records of philosophical and mystical penetration into spiritual truth, and those of the religions of Semitic origin, consisting allegedly in the Word of God to man, is not so sharp as we at first presumed. Certainly the *content* of what is claimed to be revealed differs very greatly between the religions, but if the revelation-claims of the 'Word of God' religions are treated not at their face value, but as human words, allegedly mediating divine revelation, then they become discussible and testable in the light of reason and experience just like any other claims. The contents of 'sacred scripture' then become part of the data for comparative theology.

The problems of biblical interpretation

In this section we restrict ourselves to Christian theology, and investigate the problems of biblical interpretation. But if the arguments of the last section are right, this cannot be done to the neglect of the history of religions in general and of the comparative study of other religions. Biblical interpreters must keep their eyes open to the other scriptures and the rival revelation-claims in world religion.

Certain practical problems arise at this point. The material is too vast for any one student to handle, even in a lifetime. The accumulation of scholarly work points in the other direction to increased specialisation rather than to comparative study in a wider context. This problem is illustrated by the question whether the student of theology ought always to learn Hebrew and Greek, in order to study the Old and New Testaments. Particular nuances of meaning and general categories or even climates of thought are lost if one relies solely on translations. But by parity of reasoning, the student of comparative theology ought also to learn Sanskrit, Pali and Arabic, to mention

The problems of theology

but three of the languages of sacred scripture, and few will be able to take all that in their stride. In theology more than in any other discipline, we have to learn to make do with secondary sources and utilise the research of others, simply because of the vastness of the relevant data.

Some linguistic skill, however, is desirable, not just for the purpose of using commentaries and dictionaries, but for a deeper reason. A student's whole approach to theology is impoverished if he operates only within a single language, namely his own. The universal significance of many of the concepts and ideas with which the student of theology and of the Bible is concerned is not adequately grasped when expressed solely in the medium, say, of English. A knowledge of other languages enables one – in a certain measure – to transcend the limitations of a single viewpoint, and to recognise at once the relativity of each response to an alleged transcendent reality. Familiarity with different languages and cultures helps the student to remain aware of the gap between different forms of expression and that to which they point.

The last two hundred years have seen the emergence and development of critical study of the Bible. Methods have been evolved and tested for disentangling the various strands that have gone into the composition of the different books of the Bible, dating them and reconstructing their original context. As far as the Old Testament is concerned, this has enabled the biblical scholar to get a much more accurate grasp of the different traditions and the developing faith of ancient Israel. We have learned how older and later elements, incorporating legends, folk memories and legal codes, have gone into the composition of the Pentateuch – the first five books of the Old Testament. We have learned to recognise the brilliant court history of King David's time and to distinguish the interpreting hand of the 'deuteronomic historian' behind the story of the kings of Israel and Judah.

The Psalms have been classified according to their different types and their setting in the cultic practice of the Temple at Jerusalem tentatively reconstructed. The teaching of the great prophets has been recovered from amongst the later additions of their respective followers and their contribution towards the development of a universal monotheism has been recognised. The transformation of the religion of Israel into 'late Judaism', largely as a result of the Babylonian exile, has been widely studied, and the importance of the growth of 'Messianic' hopes in the context of 'apocalyptic' expectations stressed. ('Apocalyptic' is the vivid pictorial 'uncovering' of the 'last things' – the end of the world, God's final judgement and vindication of his people.)

As far as the New Testament is concerned, a number of different methods of study have thrown considerable light on the gospels. 'Source criticism' has helped us to reconstruct the literary history of the gospels as we have them, establishing (in the eyes of most scholars) the priority of Mark, the common use by Matthew and Luke of Mark and another written source, plus written or oral sources of their own, and, much more controversially, the mixture of written and oral sources and free-style theological reflection in the case of John. 'Form criticism' has enabled us to press back to the units of oral tradition that lie behind the written gospels and see them at least in the context of the early Christian preaching, if not in the life of Jesus himself. 'Redaction criticism' has enabled us to see the mind of each evangelist at work shaping his material into a coherent whole, in the light of very definite theological views. Most obviously true of John, this has come to be recognised in the other gospel writers as well. The development of Paul's thought, as we trace it in his letters, the different perspectives of the other New Testament authors, their dominant ideas and conceptions of what God had done in Christ, are also being reconstructed and the way in which the early Christians took over late Jewish apocalyptic and moulded it to express specifically Christian expectations has been particularly emphasised.

All this work raises innumerable problems for the student of the Bible, but it represents only the first stage in the task of biblical interpretation. We can think of biblical interpretation as a twofold task, the task of exegesis and the task of hermeneutics. Exegesis is the careful reconstruction of the intention of the biblical authors and of the meaning which their writings had for the communities of ancient Israel and early Christianity. Hermeneutics is the wider task of interpreting the *real* meaning of the biblical writings, including their meaning for today. (Sometimes the word 'hermeneutics' is used to cover both stages of interpretation, but we shall keep it for the wider task of interpretation for today, by contrast with the narrower task of historical interpretation or exegesis of the texts.) All that has been said in this section so far has been about methods of exegesis, the study of the writers in their own world, the recovery of their ideas and their experience as they understood it, the manner of their appropriation of the traditions in which they stood, and the reconstruction of the historical events and developments with which they were concerned.

Clearly the detailed exegetical work which we have been talking about can be undertaken by anyone, irrespective of his own religious or non-religious beliefs. It can be undertaken phenomenologically, in the sense of historical phenomenology already discussed (pp. 28–9, above). With sufficient sympathy and discipline, it is possible to make an 'objective' study of what other people have believed, even if one does not share their world-view. But what about the second task, that of hermeneutics? The phenomenological approach seems out of place here, since we are now asking, concerning these texts, what was *really* going on, whether the authors *rightly* understood themselves and their experiences, and what, if any, is the *real* significance of their writings for today. Even so, it should be possible to maintain the hypothetical approach commended in Chapter 1. In hermeneutics, the theologian, *qua* theologian, is investigating the *claim* that the ancient texts bear witness to transcendent reality. He still need not be presupposing faith. No doubt the believing theologian will be asking straightforwardly, What is the meaning of the Bible for today? His agnostic colleague will be examining the claim that it has a meaning for today and what that meaning might be.

Before going on to discuss the problems of hermeneutics, we ought to pause to ask whether this distinction between reconstructing the biblical authors' thought and investigating attempts to understand it for today is as clear-cut as has been suggested. The distinction appears blurred in the many attempts to spell out a theology of the Old Testament or of the New. But the discipline known as 'biblical theology' has tended to impose an artificial unity on the variegated views and attitudes of the different biblical authors. Certainly, viewed phenomenologically, the developing faith of Israel has a number of distinctive features, as do the life and faith of the early Christian communities. But the major figures, such as the second Isaiah, Paul and John, have very different ways of expressing and reformulating the traditions in which they stand. To try to extract an Old Testament view of this, or a New Testament doctrine of that, is to obscure the particularity and the humanity of the individual writers. It is, at best, a hermeneutical move, claiming an underlying unity to which all these men were bearing witness, at worst, an unhistorical conflation of different human responses – perhaps on the fundamentalist premise that the real author of all these books was God.

The question of the unity of the Bible or of the Old or New Testament is ultimately a question for hermeneutics, not for exegesis. It cannot be finally answered in phenomenological terms. Whether or not there is a single underlying reality which gives unity to the variegated witness of the biblical authors is not just a historical question; it is a theological question with a bearing on religion today.

So we turn to the task of hermeneutics. An example will make clear what is involved in an attempt to interpret the Bible for today. The German New Testament scholar and theologian, Rudolf Bultmann (1884–1976), firmly believed that the New Testament preaching could confront men and women today with the living 'Word' of God. But he held that this gospel cannot be heard aright if it is expressed without further ado in the language of the various New Testament writers. For all their differences, and Bultmann was especially aware of the distinctiveness of the viewpoints of Paul and John, they shared a world-view very different from our own. The truths which they grasped were consequently expressed in a way not readily intelligible to twentieth-century, post-Enlightenment men and women. We find them hedged about with primitive elements – demons, miracles, a 'three-decker universe' of heaven, earth and hell – which create impenetrable barriers for the modern mind. So, Bultmann thought, the task of hermeneutics is to extract the real message from its primitive setting and present its message pure and untrammelled by mythology. Clearly if one is to do this there must be some principle which we can see to be applicable both to the men of the first century and to ourselves, by reference to which the essence of Christianity can be identified and re-expressed for today. If there were no connection at all between the first century and ourselves, then no first-century gospel could be gospel or revelation for the twentieth century. Bultmann held that there are indeed connections and continuities: there is on the one hand our common humanity and on the other hand the reality of God and God's claim on us. Transcending historical and cultural differences there are common factors determining what it is to be a human being in relation to God. In so far as we can see the gospel as a message which creates authentic human existence in any age, then we have the basis for interpretation for today. This is Bultmann's method of existentialist interpretation which has come to loom so large in modern Christian theology.*

Bultmann's principle of existential interpretation is a clear example of modern Christian hermeneutics and it has been widely discussed. It has much to be said for it, from the point of view of the believing Christian theologian. It involves the recognition of substantial difficulties in the world-view of the Bible, and yet it shows how those ancient texts can still be personally and religiously significant for modern men and women. On any view, an interpretation of Christianity for today must involve existential force. An interpretation that cannot be applied and lived existentially has no chance of winning assent. Moreover Bultmann's view is more faithful to Christianity as a historical religion than that of eighteenth-century writers who wanted simply to extract from the Christian story certain general moral and rational principles.

Nevertheless it has been widely held that Bultmann's approach fails to do justice to the characteristic Christian beliefs. The Christian tradition has been built up over the centuries on the supposition that the books of the Bible bear witness to certain unique and decisive acts of God within a particular strand of human history. Bultmann treats all of this as 'mythological', that is, as expressing, in this-wordly pictorial form, a deep existential truth about man's dependence on divine grace.† But this is to concede the whole material and historical world to the

---

* See R. Bultmann, *Jesus Christ and Mythology*, English trans. (London: SCM Press, 1960).
† On 'myth', see, further, pp. 144–8, below.

scientist and secular historian, to treat the world as closed and self explanatory, save only at the point of human self-understanding. Revelation, on this view, cannot occur in the physical world nor in particular historical events, but only in the mind and heart of the believer.

Bultmann has very little to say about other world religions, though he is quite happy to identify the connections between Christian 'mythological' ideas and the other religions of the ancient Middle East. In fact he seems to think that the Christian experience of authentic existence in response to the message of God's grace is unique and self-authenticating. But, in principle, it should be possible to apply this kind of hermeneutical principle to other religions, and to give them an existential interpretation too. For clearly men and women in the context of Hinduism, Buddhism and Islam, to consider only the most widespread examples, find what to them is authentic and existentially creative religious experience in their own traditions.

The example of Bultmann's hermeneutics raises the question, once again, of where revelation is to be found. Christian theological critics of Bultmann have found themselves re-examining the biblical and Christian traditions in order to see whether Bultmann's restriction of revelation to the 'existential moment' is really justified, or whether there is not a case for locating revelation in history after all.

The location of revelation

The two main problems concerning revelation, for the Christian theologian who is prepared to examine his own tradition with genuine critical rigour, in the light of rival revelation-claims from the other religious traditions, are these: Are there sufficient grounds for thinking that there has or have been some special revelation or revelations from God to man, over and above the general revelation mediated in all the religions through rational reflection, mystical experience or the sense of the holy? And if so, Where precisely is this special revelation to be found?

We have seen the difficulty of locating such revelation simply in a sacred book. There are many such books, containing conflicting claims, and their authors always turn out, on critical investigation, to be all too human and culturally conditioned. The temptation is at once to go to the other extreme and locate special revelation somehow in the believing mind or the present religious experience of those who inherit and appropriate for themselves a particular religious tradition such as Christianity.

There are, however, other possibilities which have to be explored. One such possibility is that despite the limited awareness and cultural relativity of the compilers, editors and authors of the books of the Bible, they can nevertheless be construed as bearing very varied witness to certain crucial historical events, in which the nature and will of God were decisively disclosed. Traditionally, Christianity has taught that the developing faith of Israel provided the historical and religious context in which God himself, without ceasing to be God, entered within his own creation and made himself personally known for the salvation of mankind. In the final chapter (pp. 152–7, below), we shall have something to say about the rationality of this Christian doctrine of the incarnation and of the concept of God which goes with it. Clearly one of the most important questions raised by such a view is that of the uniqueness of Jesus Christ. Can a religion which sees in him the sole and definitive presence and act of God incarnate so articulate its view of God, man and the world as to make sense of the whole history of man, including the history of other religions? In Chapter 2, reference was made to the views of John

Hick that God's special revelation of himself in Jesus cannot be thought of as the sole or normative special revelation. Equally valid revelations of the many-sided divine reality were given through other major religious figures, such as the Hindu sages, the Buddha and Muhammad. On such a view, the doctrine of the incarnation has to be jettisoned or regarded as no more than a mythological way of expressing the superlatively great religious significance of Jesus for Christians. For them he is *the* source of authentic knowledge of God. But, according to Hick, theologians have to recognise that other figures constitute, for men and women in other traditions, equally profound sources of religious experience and knowledge of the divine. Against this relativistic view, it has been argued that the case for Christian belief in Jesus Christ as the unique incarnation of God (in one of his own inner modes of being) here in our midst as one of us, has neither been refuted nor seen in its full significance by Hick. It is a prime task of Christian theology today to set out and test the grounds for thinking that the notion of revelation through incarnation represents the culmination of the idea of revelation in the history of religions, and that the historical, experiential and rational evidence are sufficient to justify the belief that, over and above God's manifold self-revelation in general, Jesus Christ is *the* place in history where God's special personal self-revelation is located. This belief cannot be justified simply by appeal to authorities – the Bible or the teaching of the Church. Only if the actual content of that witness and that teaching can be seen to make greater moral, religious and rational sense of man in his total situation than any other view will the Christian theologian have succeeded in establishing the view that Jesus is the place of revelation.

Phenomenologically speaking, it might appear that the revelation-claims of the great theistic religions follow a similar pattern – a divine message entrusted to an inspired prophet and written down in a sacred book. But when we look at the diverse writings of the Old and New Testaments and at what Christian theology has made of them, we recognise that something rather different is being postulated – a historical revelation culminating in the life, death and resurrection of a particular man. In other words, for Christians, *history* is the location of revelation. This view plunges us at once into the problems of belief and history, which are the topic of the next chapter.

Before turning to those problems, we need to pause and reflect more generally on what it means to locate special revelation in a particular book, tradition or strand of history, rather than in human religious experience in general. We considered earlier in this chapter the mistaken idea that revelation and reason were rival or complementary sources of the knowledge of God, and we showed how the distinction between natural and revealed theology tends to break down when specific revelation-claims, just as much as any other elements in human experience, are subject to critical scrutiny. But of course the actual content of any revelation-claim may well be something distinctive and new, by contrast with our general experience of the world. This is particularly true of the suggestion that special revelation is to be found in a specific slice of human history. This introduces a genuine novelty into the mass of data on which critical theology must work.

6

Theology and history

All the world religions are historical in one sense, in that
each has a long history and has developed and ramified
over the centuries. Some, such as Confucianism, Christianity and Islam, go back to a particular historical
founder; while others, such as Hinduism, have unknown
roots, long before recorded history. We know quite a lot
about some of the founders of the religions. Jesus and
Muhammad, for example, are pretty well documented,
even though, in the case of Jesus, the facts have been
overlaid to some extent by legends. Similarly we know a
great deal about the early history of Christianity and
Islam. The Buddha, by contrast, is a more shadowy
figure, and it is difficult to extract from the Pali texts and
other Buddhist scriptures a reliable historical core, from
which to reconstruct the life of the Buddha and the early
history of Buddhism.* Other founders of religions are
even more obscure. It is not at all clear, for example, even
in which century the historical Zoroaster lived. Nevertheless, in order to understand any of the world religions,
we need to know something about its early stages, enshrined in its scriptures, and about its historical development. As we saw in Chapter 2, an accurate
phenomenology of religion has to be historical, if one is
to appreciate the particular context and development of
a religion's characteristic beliefs and practices.

In another sense, however, by no means all the world
religions can be thought of as historical. There is a
marked contrast between those religions for which

* See E. J. Thomas, *The Life of the Buddha* (London: Routledge and
Kegan Paul, 1927).

history is of no great significance and those for which history itself is an important and essential factor. In two respects is this the case. Firstly, the religions differ as to how important it is to be able to know the facts about the founder. For Buddhism what matters is the teaching ascribed to the Buddha – the Four Noble (or Supreme) Truths and the Noble Eightfold Path. It does not matter that the Buddha's life is obscured now by pious legends. For Christianity, however, the life and death of Jesus are of absolutely central importance; for they are held to constitute the decisive revelatory act of God in human history for the world's salvation. Secondly, the religions differ in their views of history itself. In Hinduism the world process is thought of as cyclical and human life as an endless round of rebirth. What matters is the quest for release from this eternal recurrence. For Judaism and Christianity (and to a lesser extent Islam) the history of the world is rather a single linear process, leading in a particular direction to a specific goal or consummation. It is within the Judaeo-Christian tradition, indeed, that this conception of the historical nature of reality first arose.

It is difficult to exaggerate the importance of these differences, though they can be expressed too crudely. It is perfectly true that the eastern religions do speak of particular historical manifestations of the eternal truths or of the divine succour; the Hindu Avatār belief in repeated incarnations of God in times of special need is an example of this. It is also true that Judaism and Christianity can stress the recurrent blessing of God through the seasons or the timeless teaching of the Torah or of the Sermon on the Mount (though at some cost here to the real context of Jesus' teaching), and there is, of course, the more mystical side to Judaism, Christianity and Islam. But the fact remains that the dominant pattern in eastern religion is that of the quest for mystical or devotional release from a recurring state of bondage, while the dominant thrust of the Judaeo-Christian tradition is towards construing human history as moving under divine providence towards a particular goal. Moreover, for the religions of Semitic origin, it is particular acts of God in history that reveal to mankind the nature, significance and goal of history, and constitute the means by which men and women can come to share in the power of that future.

Clearly these differences greatly affect the value placed on present religious experience. The least historical religions are those which place the most stress on mystical experience, and teach the view that mystical experience is the essence of religion. We think here of the serene nature mysticism of Taoism, the enlightenment sought in Theravada Buddhism, and the various schools of philosophical Hinduism, where release is sought through the mystical knowledge of the soul's identity with Ultimate Reality or Brahman. Even where mystical experience is thought of in more personal terms, as in the Bhagavad Gītā, the stress remains on the present spiritual blessedness enjoyed by the devotee. The historical religions do not ignore the experiential dimension and, as we have noted, they can embrace the possibility of mysticism, but the emphasis lies more on the saving acts of God and the will of God for the future.

We shall see in the next chapter how even the mystical types of eastern religion are at the same time permeated by an intense ethical concern. This ethical dimension becomes more personal in the context of devotional religion, where the right and the good are thought of in terms of the nature and will of God. But we shall also see that a range of different attitudes towards morality corresponds with the less or more historical nature of the religions, the less historical tending to teach a timeless pattern of righteousness or compassion, the more historical tending to demand a progressive realisation of God's ultimate plan for the world.

Theology and history

In personal theism, the characteristic mode of religious experience is not so much mystical experience as the numinous experience of awe and abasement before the holy and righteous God. It is this sense of otherness rather than identity that provides the impetus towards the notion of a transformation of the human world in accordance with the will of God. The historical religions tend to see this as a historical task, even though they hold that the ultimate destiny of man can only be realised through God's own acts. The greatest stress, then, in the historical religions is much more on the acts of God himself and on expectations of historical change under God's providence than on present religious experience, however important that experience may be to the individual believer.

It will be evident that history is much more of a problem for the theologian who stands in the Judaeo-Christian tradition than for his eastern colleagues. To speak of God's acts in history, to see history as a goal-directed process under God, and to look for decisive historical transformations in the future, create enormous problems for the theologian, especially in an age of critical historical self-consciousness such as ours. It is not surprising that modern theologians in the west are tempted to retreat from these problems and look elsewhere for the essence of Christianity. Thus we find, as a strand in modern Christian theology, an almost eastern stress on religious experience after all.

Christianity's dependence on history

If, for the rest of this chapter, we concentrate on Christian theology, it is because these problems are peculiarly acute for Christianity. In addition to the beliefs which Christianity shares with Judaism about God's providential fashioning of a particular people in history to be the recipients of his revelation of himself, precisely in and through their peculiar history and experience, Christianity has taught further, as we saw in the last chapter, that that revelation culminated in the incarnation – the life, death and resurrection of Jesus being construed as God's own personal presence and action within the structures of creation and of historical human existence.

In the past, this remarkable doctrine led to very exclusive claims for faith in Jesus Christ as the only path to salvation and the knowledge of God. Most modern Christian theologians are aware of the morally dubious nature of such exclusive claims, given the large number of people who have lived before Christ or outside Christianity's sphere of influence. They now tend to admit that knowledge of God is not restricted to human response to Jesus Christ. But, unless they have abandoned the doctrine of the incarnation altogether, they are bound to continue to hold that God's personal presence and action in human form in Jesus Christ have provided a way of closer, more personal knowledge of God than is available elsewhere. They are also liable to hold that whatever knowledge and experience of God *are* available through other faiths will eventually, in God's future, no doubt for many beyond the grave, be enhanced and transformed by encounter with the risen Christ as *the* human face of God.

The point which we need to notice here about these characteristic Christian beliefs concerning the significance of Jesus Christ is how much they make Christianity dependent on a particular slice of human history. If God's self-disclosure is pivoted upon a historical incarnation, then the relation between man and God for all eternity depends upon what happened in Palestine nearly two thousand years ago. This is the 'scandal of particularity' which has so often proved a stumbling block even to sympathetic observers of Christianity. There are, as we shall see, grave philosophical difficulties about the very notion of a particular divine act in history, but quite apart from this problem, many more specific difficulties have been raised, of which the two most important are these: How can the ultimate destiny of all men be dependent on the life and death of a particular man in an obscure corner of the ancient Middle East? And, given the uncertainties of historical knowledge, can we ever hope to acquire sufficiently certain information about Jesus to sustain, let alone demand, the interpretation which Christian doctrine has placed upon him?

The first difficulty was felt very strongly in the eighteenth century, the time of the Enlightenment. The German dramatist and critic, Gotthold Ephraim Lessing (1729–81), put the matter thus: 'Accidental truths of history can never become the proof of necessary truths of reason.'* The implication of this objection is that only something in principle available to all – the 'necessary truths of reason' – can carry the weight of absolute and eternal significance. The philosopher, Fichte, brought this implication out when he said 'only the metaphysical can save, never the historical'. Earlier Kant had, in a similar way, disparaged the historical in favour of the ethical. For Kant, ethical demands are among the necessary truths of reason, since they reflect man's universal rational nature. It might be the case that a particular man had, as a matter of fact, brought to our attention these sublime rational or ethical truths, but once recognised they stood on their own feet, as it were, and required no continuing support by reference to history.

It was not very difficult for Christian theology to answer objections expressed in these eighteenth-century terms. The premise of the objection, namely, the view that only the metaphysical or the ethical could save, could simply be denied. On the contrary, it was the

---

* 'On the Proof of the Spirit and of Power', in *Lessing's Theological Writings*, ed. Henry Chadwick (London: A. & C. Black, 1956), p. 53.

characteristic belief of Christianity that the human predicament was such that only divine action from outside could bring about the necessary transformation. But the question why there was need of such a particular, localised, historical action remained, and Christian thinkers in the nineteenth and twentieth centuries have been peculiarly sensitive to it. In the nineteenth century, the Danish philospher, Soren Kierkegaard (1813–55), attempted to bridge the gap between the Jesus of history and the present by speaking of a faith-relation in which Jesus becomes the contemporary of each believer, irrespective of historical enquiry. In the twentieth century, Rudolf Bultmann, as we saw in the last chapter, has proposed a similar mode of existential interpretation, which purports to free the faith-response to Christian preaching from any dependence on uncertain historical facts.

Most Christian theologians have not been happy with these suggestions, however. We recall the difficulty felt by many over Bultmann's restriction of authentic existence to the Christian response to Christ. Once Christianity's dependence on unique historical events has been broken, it seems arbitrary to accord a higher place to Christian existential claims than to those of any other experiential faith. On the contrary, the traditional claim of Christianity to absoluteness rested precisely on the alleged fact of God's own unique involvement with humanity in person in the man Jesus. The moral and religious force of Christian incarnational belief was held to be contained precisely in the fact that 'God so loved the world that he sent his only-begotten Son . . .'* or, to put the matter in other words, that God, out of love for mankind, made himself vulnerable to evil and death, through sharing the human condition himself at a particular point in time. Admittedly, Christian theologians

* John 3.16.

went on to speak of the resurrection, and of the continuing spiritual and sacramental presence and activity of the risen Christ, thus themselves bridging the gap between past and present. But the main-stream Christian tradition has, so far, refused to part with the 'scandal of particularity' and its belief in a historical incarnation.

The quest of the historical Jesus

The burden of the last section was that most Christian theologians and indeed most Christians have not felt able to abandon Christianity's links with a particular slice of history, and this now brings us to the second difficulty, the uncertainty of the actual historical facts about Jesus. We have already said something in Chapters 1 and 5 about the impact of the use of critical historical methods upon the Christian Bible. Once the documents on which Christians rely for their knowledge of Jesus were subjected to critical investigation, it was discovered how much they reflected the post-Easter faith of the early Christian communities, and how much the stories had been embellished in the course of telling, before they were written down. In the nineteenth century, many attempts were made to reconstruct the purely human story of the life of the man Jesus. The most famous of these was *The Life of Jesus* by the French historian, Ernst Renan (1823–92). At the beginning of the twentieth century, Albert Schweitzer (1875–1965) examined such lives of Jesus in his book *The Quest of the Historical Jesus*, and showed conclusively that they were all failures, reflecting the presuppositions and attitudes of their authors. In a well-known image, each had looked down a deep well and discerned only his own reflection at the bottom. Notwithstanding this criticism, Schweitzer himself attempted to draw a picture of Jesus. His Jesus was a bizarre figure, obsessed by apocalyptic imagery and going to his death in a vain attempt to force God's hand. At least Schweitzer avoided

The problems of theology

the danger of a disguised self-portrayal, but his picture of Jesus failed to convince, and the more common reaction was to conclude that we simply do not have the evidence on which to reconstruct the life of Jesus.

This sceptical conclusion was accepted by Rudolf Bultmann and built into his theology, which, as we have seen, divorces faith from history, and treats the faith of the believer as the real point of contact between God and the world.

Bultmann's own pupils, recognising that more justice must be done to the content of the preaching which evokes faith, have reinvestigated the evidence and begun a 'new quest of the historical Jesus'. They have urged that it is possible to reconstruct the salient features of the life and teaching of Jesus, so that real continuity can be shown between Christian faith today and the faith of Jesus himself, which, they hold, was the starting point and impetus for specifically Christian experience.

Despite the fact that, for over a hundred and fifty years, Protestant Christian theology has, at least in one of its strands, followed Schleiermacher in making Jesus' unique God-consciousness the basis and the source of Christian experience of God, it has to be admitted that the 'new questers', in concentrating on the faith of Jesus, have singled out the most uncertain element in the whole reconstruction. Even if we can get a reliable picture of the life and teaching of Jesus, and even if this necessarily includes some idea of his striking sense of oneness with the Father, the actual self-consciousness of Jesus is bound to be the least accessible part of the picture to the critical historian.

This brief survey of the difficulties which Christian theologians have encountered in their attempts to reconstruct the life of Jesus by critical historical methods suggests that the whole enterprise may have been begun on the wrong footing. One reaction, that of conservative Christian theology, is to reject the critical approach and return to the Bible as it stands as somehow divinely guaranteed. But we have already seen how difficult it is to fence off any area of enquiry in this way. Another and more plausible reaction is to refuse to restrict the historical enquiry to the quest for the purely human Jesus, and admit that, if the critical historian refrains from prejudging the matter, he may himself uncover something here that bursts the bounds of normal human categories. After all, among the data to be considered in investigating the figure of Jesus is the remarkable reaction to his life and death that occurred so rapidly and led to the kind of 'high Christology' found in the New Testament documents. The historian cannot just ignore the evidence for the resurrection, however hard it may be to handle. The Easter faith, the empty tomb, the rapid rise of Christianity, the forms of religious experience which it engendered, and the concepts fashioned so soon by Paul and John and the others to account for what had happened – all this is part of the data with which the historian has to come to terms. Nor, as has been admitted by the 'new questers', have the actual life and teaching of Jesus vanished behind the screen of the post-resurrection faith.

Christian theology today may well conclude that a critical reconstruction of the life and teaching of Jesus in the light of the impact which he made on his immediate followers and on the communities that arose after his death and alleged resurrection is not as difficult a task as it was made out to be by scholars who felt that they had to discount the Easter faith. Such a reconstruction, however, is bound still to be tentative and provisional, and there is not likely to be universal agreement even about its main features. The problem remains, therefore, for Christian theology, that once its sources are subjected to critical enquiry, even if the results are much more positive than at first seemed likely, it is still vulnerable to uncertainty and reinterpretation.

On the other hand it might be argued that Christian

theology can at least appeal to real history and not to some alleged divinely guaranteed account. Once the sources are permitted to be investigated critically, the risks of disintegration are certainly greatly increased, but so are the possibilities of public historical argument, pointing to features in the records of the life of Jesus and the rise of Christianity that cry out for some adequate explanation.

Church history

The historical religions, that is, those which regard all human history as a significant process under God, are clearly going to pay much more attention to their own history and developments, and to see them as religiously significant, than are those ahistorical religions which commend a timeless way of righteousness or salvation. Not that developments in other faiths are to be ignored. On the contrary the strength and potential of any religion consists largely of its ability to develop in relation to increased human knowledge and increased awareness of other religions. It is always a mistake in comparative theology to take a particular version of any one religion's self-understanding as fixed and fossilised. Nevertheless the historical religions do have a special interest in seeing the hand of providence behind their own history and developments. Christianity has never regarded the incarnation as an isolated divine act in the past. Central as its faith in the divinity of Christ has been, it has always regarded the incarnation as the culmination of a long period of preparation. Similarly the reception of Jesus as the divine–human revealer and saviour by the growing body of Christians, freed from the confines of a particular nation, was construed as itself taking place under God's providence. The history of the Christian Church came to be regarded as God's providential work, by which his saving acts and future purpose were made known. The growing Church itself was regarded as the first-fruits of the kingdom of God.

An important example can be drawn from early church history, the period of the first four or five centuries, in which the characteristic shape of Christian belief in the Trinity and incarnation, as expressed in the Christian creeds, was being hammered out. (These were the times of the men known as the 'Fathers of the Church', and the discipline which studies them is known as 'patristics'.) Christian theology may see this period as a period of struggle, under the providence of God, for an adequate expression, so far as human language permits, of what was revealed in the events concerning Jesus. The historian, however, will be very conscious of the political struggles involved and of the use made in disputes with the so-called 'heretics' of philosophical terminology apparently quite alien to the thought-world of the Bible. He will also be conscious of the limited and relative nature of the whole culture and world-view of the Fathers, as indeed of the men of the New Testament. Something has already been said about this problem in the last chapter and we shall return to it below. But in the light of all these difficulties, it is apparent how problematic is the Christian theological claim to discern in the early councils and creeds a permanent and normative insight into the nature and acts of God.

On the other hand justice must be done by the historian to what actually came out of those often sordid struggles. The historian may become so much aware of the dubious nature of some of the arguments used and of some of the factors involved in the Christological and trinitarian disputes that he may fail to see the religiously creative potential of what in fact emerged. Or he may himself become the victim of a kind of negative theological bias. An example of this is the view of Professor Maurice Wiles that only an interpretation absolutely required

by the evidence can be admitted in Christian theology.*
This principle of economy, as has been pointed out (pp.
40–1, above), can distort historical judgement and blind
the critic to the scope and originality of what admittedly
has emerged in a rather messy way. We shall return to
these points in the final chapter.

Similar considerations need to be borne in mind by the
Christian theologian in his study of later church history.
So conscious is he, *qua* historian, of the all too human
factors shaping the medieval Church, the Reformation,
the missionary expansions and the modern ecumenical
movement, that he will be inclined to give a secular
account of these developments in purely human terms.
Such accounts are not to be despised any more than are
sociological accounts of the hidden causes influencing
church and sect life. But just as we saw reason in Chapter
3 to limit the scope of sociological study to certain
aspects of religion, so should the theologian now ask his
colleagues to reckon with the possibility that the course
of church history is not to be explained wholly in terms
of the categories of ordinary secular history. This is not
just to plead that justice must be done to the religious
consciousness as a factor in human history. That might
itself be just one among many purely human elements in
the complex story of man. The theologian will be speaking about the possibility of construing church history in
terms of divine providence, working in and through
pretty recalcitrant human material, for the unification of
mankind in response to God's self-revelation. Admittedly, it looks much less plausible than it did in the case of
the historical Jesus to suppose that the story of the Christian Church is a more than human story. It is not only a
question of secular political factors often determining
the events. There is the much greater problem of the cor-

* *The Remaking of Christian Doctrine* (London: SCM Press, 1974),
p.18.

114

ruptions and evils that stand out only too clearly in a survey of the record of the Church. On the other hand the historian has to reckon with the men whom the Christian Church calls saints, with the potentialities in Christianity for reformation and renewal despite its failures and corruptions, and with its actual and potential unifying power in the history of mankind.*

This specifically Christian view of the history of the Christian Church is widely felt today by Christian theologians themselves to be liable to narrow down the sphere of divine action too exclusively. Just as the history of Israel and the emergence of Christianity are to be seen in their wider context in the history of religions, so the history of the Church must be regarded, theologically speaking, as but one strand in the whole divine–human encounter. Christian theologians are much more disposed than they were to see the hand of God at work in other religions too, and to regard the encounter of religions in the modern world as itself providential. The emergence and spread of Islam, long after the rise of Christianity, is only the most notable counter-example to a too facile Christian reading of divine providence in history.

There is not space here to discuss the vast amount of material and the innumerable problems which concern the student of church history down the centuries. But a little more must be said about the use of historical method, and the philosophy that often accompanies it.

Modern historical method

The methods of modern critical history, when applied to the books of the Bible and to the records of the Christian

---

* See W. Pannenberg, *Faith and Reality*, English trans. (London: Search Press, and Philadelphia: Westminster Press, 1977), chs. 8 and 9.

past, have affected Christian theology more profoundly than any purely scientific discoveries or hypotheses, such as the theory of evolution. The change that has come over Christianity in the last two centuries as its theologians and leaders have had to grapple with the effect of such critical study is probably the greatest transformation and development in its long history. The process is certainly not complete, and it may never be completed, since resistance to the applications of critical methods, especially to the Bible, is a deeply felt religious reaction, and a conservative anti-critical Christian theology is likely to remain a permanent feature of the Christian scene. It is interesting to speculate how far Islam will be able to achieve comparable developments, as critical methods are applied to the Qu'ran. The pressure to apply them will surely become irresistible. It is only the fact that Christianity was so much involved in the history of the European Enlightenment that made it necessary for Christianity to face these problems rather earlier than the other religions. The resistance, in the Islamic world, however, to the critical study of the Qu'ran is likely to be much more powerful than Christian resistance to critical study of the Bible, since the Qu'ran is given an even higher status in Islam than the Bible is in Christianity. Even when the Bible has been thought of as divinely guaranteed, it has been understood to be pointing away from itself to Christ. But for Muslims the Qu'ran is itself God's revelation. On the other hand, the Qu'ran is not so complicated a book as the Bible. It does not come from many different hands over many centuries.

Christian resistance to the subjection of the sources of Christianity to historical criticism is not only understandable as a religious reaction. It is also understandable in face of the extravagances of the early critics. We have already seen how an excessive scepticism has tended to characterise their approach, even down to the present day. It is often pointed out how much more positive are the results reached by historians of the ancient Greek and Roman worlds, working sometimes on more fragmentary records than those concerning the birth of Christianity. It is also worth pointing out that a Christian theologian who thinks that he has worked out a theological method of bypassing the question of historical evidence is likely to become somewhat blasé and cavalier in his historical scepticism. The danger of bias works both ways. Traditional Christian theology may have a vested interest in positive reliable results, but it is also true that existentialist theology may induce a careless attitude to the evidence or even a desire to outdo the secular historian in scepticism.

A further problem has affected the readiness of Christian theologians to accept the critical methods of modern historiography. Especially in the nineteenth century, the critical approach was heavily conditioned by a variety of philosophical presuppositions. Much of the disrepute which the so-called 'higher criticism' in Germany brought upon the whole idea of biblical criticism was due to D. F. Strauss's notorious book *The Life of Jesus* (1835). But Strauss was a leading disciple of Hegel and his approach to the sources was far more determined by his philosophical bias than by purely historical method. At the opposite end of the philosophical spectrum, much nineteenth-century historiography was conditioned by 'positivist' attempts to assimilate the human to the natural sciences. If the leading motive of historical investigation was to explain all phenomena in terms of general laws, it is not surprising that anything unique or extraordinary should tend to be explained away. The spirit of positivism affected much historical writing that could hardly be classified as fully or explicitly positivist in intention. We have already referred to Renan's *Life of Jesus*. It was basically a philosophical decision on Renan's part to exclude the supernatural from consideration.

The problems of theology

Of course, the historian is rightly suspicious of supernatural claims. 'Miracle' is not a category to which he can readily turn. It has to be admitted that belief in miracles was common in the ancient world and characteristic of all the religions of the world, especially in their more primitive stages. In pre-scientific times, extraordinary events, whose causes were unknown, were readily attributed to direct divine intervention. But it is one thing to exercise a healthy scepticism in dealing with miracle stories in the gospels. It is quite another to exclude all reference to divine action and divine revelation in writing a historical account of Jesus. To conclude that God does not (usually) act by miraculous intervention may be a sensible judgement in the light of all the relevant considerations. To presume that God does not act at all is a philosophical presupposition, as, of course, is the assumption that God does not exist at all. These remarks about the dangers of philosophical prejudice affecting the manner in which critical historical methods are handled apply just as much to the patristic and later periods of church history as they do to the life of Jesus and the apostolic age.

It should be noted here that the idea of divine action in history is a much more sophisticated theological idea than appears to the naive observer. The concept of divine providence has been spelled out very sensitively by writers in the 'Thomist' tradition in terms of the primary causality of God operating in and through the secondary causality and agency of his creatures. The miraculous is certainly not the only category in terms of which the notion of divine action may be expressed. On the contrary, the Christian tradition has held that for the most part God acts indirectly by providence rather than by miracle. That is to say, he works in and through his creatures at every level of created being. At the personal level, he wins their response and inspires their deeds without forcing the natural story of their deeds and interactions.

118

On the other hand we have no business to rule out miracle *a priori*. We have already insisted that the actual evidence for the resurrection must be examined fairly, though the Christian theologian may conclude that the resurrection is, so far, something absolutely unique, bursting the bounds of the categories both of providence and of miracle.

One of the most interesting writers on the bearing of modern historiography on Christian theology was the Heidelberg theologian and sociologist, Ernst Troeltsch (1865–1923). Troeltsch was convinced of the great difference which the rise of modern historical method had made to human self-consciousness. Modern man had come to see himself, his culture and his society as historical phenomena, interrelated and interconnected with all that had gone before. Troeltsch was not a positivist. He did not exclude the novel and the unique from the historical process. But he did insist that the new had its roots in the old and can be understood only in relation to what had gone before and what was going on around. Troeltsch advanced three criteria of historical enquiry: criticism, analogy and correlation. By these he meant that every historical phenomenon must be subjected to critical investigation, that an event can be understood only if it bears at least some analogy to comparable events elsewhere, and that no event can be understood in isolation from the surrounding and conditioning factors. None of this rules out religious claims. It is quite possible to investigate the suggestion that some historical phenomenon is the bearer of greater spiritual value than anything found elsewhere. But it does, for Troeltsch, rule out the notion of direct supernatural interventions or revelations out of the blue. Belief in such notions he calls 'naive supernaturalism' and 'naive traditionalism', characteristic of man's pre-critical, pre-historical consciousness.

Much of this is perfectly acceptable. Comparative theology today should certainly be carried out within the framework of some such historical self-consciousness. But it is surprising that such a sensitive religious thinker as Troeltsch should have confined his positive estimate of the history of religions to the emergence of spiritual value as indicative of the presence and activity of the divine spirit in human history. Wolfhart Pannenberg has pointed out that the use of Troeltsch's historical methods might itself disclose some novel historical phenomenon requiring some other religious category to do it justice. The categories of incarnational theism do not have to be applied in a naive supernaturalist way. The Christian theologian might still be able to claim that the history of Jesus, for all its continuity and correlation with what had gone before, is best understood in incarnational terms. Similarly the history of Christianity might still be best understood in providential terms. Even the resurrection, despite its unparalleled nature in the history of the world, was not without connections with the eschatological hopes and expectations of late Judaism.

Historical relativism and Christian theology

Our discussion of Troeltsch has omitted one aspect of his view of history which has had an even more disquieting effect on Christian theology than his rejection of naive supernaturalism. It has to be admitted that Troeltsch himself became more and more convinced of the historically relative nature of every religious position. The view that all human notions, including religious ideas, are so conditioned by the cultural framework of a particular time and place in history that no religion can have absolute and universal significance for man is becoming increasingly widely held. It ties in with parallel developments in the sociology of knowledge and the philosophy of science, which treat every view of the world as limited by and relative to the set of presuppositions accepted in a particular community.

Theology and history

There is undoubtedly some truth in all this. Historical consciousness has brought home to us how partial and conditioned are the responses of any one human community, even the scientific community, to the world. Increased knowledge of other cultures and civilisations has reinforced this sense of historical relativism. As was pointed out in Chapter 1, Christian theology has to come to terms with the alien aspects of the world-view of the late Judaism within which Christianity arose. It is impossible to transfer their world-view without further ado into our twentieth-century world. An obvious example, mentioned above, is the whole world of demonological belief, which determined the attitude of the men of biblical times, including Jesus himself, to certain types of illness. Many of the miracle stories of the Bible reflect a similar pre-scientific consciousness which cannot be appropriated as it stands. The great strength of Bultmann's theology was that he had appreciated these facts and tried to extract the kernel of Christianity from the husk of outmoded ideas.

But, as we have seen, there is much room for disagreement over what constitutes the husk and what constitutes the kernel. The temptation of Bultmann and his followers is on the one hand to exaggerate the amount that has to be discarded and on the other to accept too uncritically some such science-based modern philosophy as positivism. A similar temptation leads writers conscious of the problem of historical relativism to exaggerate the way in which a past world-view constitutes a total framework to be accepted or rejected in its entirety. Thus Dennis Nineham, in his *The Use and Abuse of the Bible*,* greatly inflates the notion of 'totality' into the conception of each historical age and community thinking and acting within a closed conceptual framework of

* London: Macmillan, 1976.

121

its own, cut off from every other, including our own. This is a great oversimplification of the way in which ideas and attitudes are acquired and transmitted. Except in the context of a primitive tribe (and even this requires qualification) men never live in sealed-off worlds of their own. Their views are never so uniform and coherent as this picture suggests. Every community includes a whole variety of conflicting philosophical views, never more so than in our own time. Moreover, as was argued in Chapter 1, there are continuities across the borders of cultural change which prevent us from being totally cut off from the men of the first century or the Middle Ages.

Two factors, in particular, militate against the idea of complete historical relativism. In the first place, we are all human beings living in the same world, and this makes for some things in common, even with the remotest past or the most distant culture. It is at least the suggestion of some of the religions of the world that mankind, for all their cultural diversity, are being fashioned into a single family by the actions and purposes of God. These may be construed very differently and very partially at different times and places; but if they are indeed the ultimate realities behind the vagaries of human history, then we should not be surprised at the idea of their imposing some unity and continuity in the life of man.

In the second place, on any view, we in the twentieth century actually stand in a relation of historical continuity with one or more of the great religious traditions of the world. Despite all the changes and transformations that have affected Christian history down the ages, the twentieth-century Christian inhabits the same strand of human history that goes back to Jesus of Nazareth and before him to the faith of Israel. For all its limitations, the Bible itself remains a powerful unifying factor in Christian history, and such may well be the providential role of the 'holy book' in the historical religions. The fact that now the world religions are constrained by twentieth-century global history to meet each other in dialogue itself calls for theological interpretation in providential terms.

7

Ethical problems

Theory and practice in religion

So far in this book we have been concerned almost entirely with theoretical problems, and especially with the
relation between theology and other subjects, such as
history, philosophy, social science and comparative religion. We have concentrated on theology's attempt to
understand, through critical study and rational reflection, the facts about God, man and the world. We shall,
in the final chapter, continue this theme by asking to
what extent, in the light of the problems discussed, it is
still possible for a religion such as Christianity to put forward doctrines to be believed.

This whole approach, however, is open to serious criticism. Reference was made at the end of Chapter 1 to the
Marxist–Leninist view that our task is not to understand
the world but to change it. This sense that practice comes
first and theory, if at all, only second, is shared by many
for whom a religion is primarily a way of life. From time
to time we have mentioned that strand in the philosophy
of religion, from Kant to Braithwaite, which sees the doctrinal element in religion as only a pictorial way of reinforcing certain ethical ideals. This is hardly true to the
phenomenological reality of the world religions, as we
have seen, but it remains the case that all religions
include a strong ethical element. Buddhism's analysis of
the human situation is made in the interests of a practical
cure. Hinduism has always taught the eternal *dharma*, a

word which means both 'righteousness' and 'religion'.*
Islam insists on a strict morality in obedience to the
revealed will of God. Christianity has always stressed
some variant on the theme that 'pure religion and unde-
filed is this, to visit the fatherless and widows in their
affliction and to keep oneself unspotted from the
world'.†

Karl Barth, whose main work lay in 'dogmatics', constantly argued that doctrinal theology must never be
separated from Christian ethics. He included a long ethical section in each part of his *Church Dogmatics*, and
went so far as to say: 'a reality which is conceived and
presented in such a way that it does not affect or claim
men or awaken them to responsibility or redeem them,
i.e. a theoretical reality, cannot possibly be the reality of
the Word of God, no matter how great may be the rich-
ness of its content or the profundity of its conception'.‡

Anyone who is prepared to put himself imaginatively
and sympathetically into the shoes of a participant in any
one of the world religions, will recognise that it is indeed
true that, for the believer, theory and practice in religion
are very closely linked. But, as we have argued all along,
the theologian may or may not be a believer, and even if
he is, he will, *qua* theologian, need to step back from his
own commitment, to reflect carefully and rationally on
the content of his faith. In doing so, he will inevitably
find himself making distinctions. He will distinguish the
different dimensions of religion.§ Among those dimensions is certainly the ethical dimension, but there is also
the doctrinal dimension; for it is characteristic of the

---

* See S. Radhakrishnan, *The Hindu View of Life* (London: Allen
and Unwin, 1927), chs. 3 and 4.

† James 1.27.

‡ *Church Dogmatics*, I, 2, English trans. (Edinburgh: T. & T. Clark,
1956), p. 793.

§ See, above, p. 26.

major religions to put forward for belief a systematic view of the world and of human life. These views differ regarding the existence and nature of God, the degree and nature of his involvement with the world, the meaning of human life and its ultimate destiny, and the resources available to man for coping with the problems of existence and realising man's goal.

It is not unreasonable that the theologian should abstract from the full reality of living religion these beliefs for special scrutiny. He is not talking, however, about 'theoretical reality'. Rather he is, for the time being, talking theoretically about the ultimate realities with which men, allegedly, have to do. No doubt he will see why, if the facts are as a given religion asserts them to be, men feel themselves bound to respond with worship and action. In so far as he spells out those other dimensions and traces their connection with and manner of dependence on the fundamental realities with which doctrine deals, he will be engaged in liturgiology and ethics. These are important disciplines, but only confusion results if they are conflated with doctrinal theology or substituted for it out of misguided enthusiasm. As we saw at the beginning, it is one thing to 'follow the way', another to think clearly about the realities claimed to determine the world and human life.

The importance of making these distinctions becomes quite clear if we take theology out of the sphere of *church* dogmatics, and pursue it in the wider contexts of debate between believer and unbeliever and of the dialogue of religions. It is important, in the dialogue situation, to know how far an ethical ideal, be it individual or social, which a particular religion fosters, is of general application, irrespective of the peculiar truth-claims of that religion, and how far it depends on the particular facts which that religion claims to obtain. To answer these questions we need to know precisely what *is* being asserted in each religion about fundamental realities, and whether those doctrines are true. Secular philosophers tend to be much clearer about this than theologians themselves. A. C. Danto in his book, *Mysticism and Morality*,* shows plainly how our assessment of the ethical ideals of a given religion must depend, to a large extent, on whether the doctrines in relation to which that ideal is spelled out are true.

No apology, then, is required for concentrating in this book on the theoretical problems of theology. In this chapter, however, we do turn our attention to the different area of the practical problems of theology, the area of theological ethics. Even here we shall still be pretty theoretical. We are not going to offer any practical maxims, nor to try to answer Lenin's penetrating question, 'What is to be done?' We shall again be standing back from any actual commitments, which we may or may not have, and asking ourselves what practical ideals the religions teach, and how they see them in relation to their fundamental doctrines. We shall press the question of how far the different religions' practical ideals conflict, and we shall offer some reflections on the relation between religious and secular ethics. Finally we shall single out the problem of the conflict between emphasis on ideals of individual life and emphasis on social ethics, and try to see where the religions stand on this much debated issue.

Comparative religious ethics

The fact that the moral teachings as well as the doctrines of the different religions may conflict has been stressed by William A. Christian in his two books, *Meaning and Truth in Religion* and *Oppositions of Religious Doctrines*, to which reference was made above (p. 39). Of

* New York: Basic Books Inc., 1972, and Harmondsworth: Penguin Books, 1976.

course it is important to try to see if there is a common core of ethical teaching in the world religions, and thus a shared basis for practical co-operation, but we should also be aware of the several ways in which their different teachings may be incompatible.

One possible incompatibility need not worry us much. It may very well be the case that the injunction to follow the Noble Eightfold Path and the injunction to observe the Jewish Torah cannot both be obeyed by one and the same person at the same time. The Jewish law contains a whole number of regulations which would be quite irrelevant and inappropriate for the Buddhist to undertake, and vice versa. But no one need worry about this. It does not follow from the fact that Judaism and Buddhism have different religious and moral ideals that they conflict in important matters such as conduct towards one's neighbour. The Jew may follow the ideal taught in his religion, and the Buddhist that in his, but find themselves co-operating, when they meet, in common concern for the poor.

The situation is different, however, if different ethical ideals are put forward as universally binding. If one religion teaches that men and women are equal, and should always be equally treated, and another teaches the subordination of women to men, then we have an irresolvable conflict. Neither will be happy to allow the other's ideal to prevail within its sphere of influence and restrict its own ideal to its own followers. Such conflicts undoubtedly occur, but the matter is complicated by the fact that the moral ideals of the different religions develop and change. I deliberately did not ascribe the conflicting views on the equality of women to specific religions such as Christianity and Islam, since both religions have shown internal conflicts and transformations on this subject. The student of comparative religious ethics will need to be aware of these developments, and what makes them possible in a given religion.

Ethical problems

One thing that makes ethical development possible is that it may take time for the implications of a religion's fundamental teachings to be drawn out. Thus St. Paul apparently taught *both* that in Christ 'there is neither slave nor free, there is neither male nor female'* *and* that 'the head of a woman is her husband'.† It has taken centuries for Christianity to realise (and the idea is still resisted) that the former view is the more lasting and the more essentially Christian.

The example of the equality of the sexes indicates another important factor, of which the student of comparative ethics must be aware. The ideals of the religions are deeply embedded in particular cultural contexts. The social conditions of the time when they were first put forward were bound to impose at least temporary limitations on their scope. The striking fact, however, is the way in which the creative religious impulses that lie behind the emergence of the world religions have it in them to transcend these socio-cultural limitations in the course of time. Consequently we should beware of evaluating some specific ethical teaching in the abstract. We have always to press the question whether it is really implied in the fundamental and essential doctrines of the religion in question.

Such considerations are highly relevant to the age-old debate between the religions of the east and of the west over their respective quietist and activist tendencies. It has often been held that the mystical element in Hinduism and Buddhism is so strong, and the ideal of contemplation and release from worldly cares so all-pervasive in the Indian tradition, that these religions are not able to foster the same concern for love and justice that the Judaeo-Christian tradition has, at least in theory, promulgated. It is an important task in compara-

* Galatians 3.28.
† 1 Corinthians 11.3.

The problems of theology

tive ethics to try to see how far these judgements are true. Buddhism has in fact strongly emphasised compassion in individual relations and a high social ethic, and seen these ideas as inseparable from the quest for enlightenment. Hinduism has in fact shown itself capable of the most remarkable reformation and participation, through such agencies as the Ramakrishna Mission, in social action, and seen these ideals as inseparable from the love of God that brings release. On the other hand, there is a strand in eastern religion, particularly in Hinduism with its tendency to subordinate the personal element in religion, towards the view that God or the Absolute lies ultimately beyond good and evil. The implications of this have been greatly over-emphasised and some would say totally misconceived by R. C. Zaehner in his last book, *Our Savage God*,* but the danger of stressing the ultimate transcendence of ethical distinctions is bound to worry the Judaeo-Christian or the Muslim mind.

Despite these differences, it may well appear to the student of comparative ethics that the religions do contain at least the potentiality of developing a common ethical core. The ideals of love and of compassion for the poor and suffering are taught in all the great faiths, and can and do lead to co-operation in social and medical work, and in pressure for a more just society. But apart from the obvious differences that remain, the student will need to scrutinise more carefully the apparently similar elements in the ethical teaching of the religions. The Christian ideal of love and the Buddhist ideal of compassion, for example, may appear to have much in common, but the question must be pressed whether these ideals are really the same. In each case the ideal must be scrutinised in detail, its exemplification in Jesus and in

* London: Collins, 1974.

the Buddha studied, its connections with all the other elements in the religions examined (including their doctrines), and its potentiality for development and application in very different cultural conditions explored. One important question is how far, in each case, the ideal provides the dynamic impulse not only for individual human goodness, but for the restructuring of human social life. It is not at all obvious that, under such deeper scrutiny, the two religions will be found to be saying the same thing.

A further factor to be taken into consideration is the manner in which the ethical ideal is held to be actually realisable in life. Is the ideal held up as something to be struggled for, under the inspiration of shining examples from the past – Jesus and the Buddha, the Christian and the Buddhist saints? Or is the gap between the actual situation in men's lives and society and the ideal which the religion envisages to be overcome some other way, not so much by struggle as by divine action in and upon men's lives? What are the resources, in other words, that the religion claims to be available for the transformation of men and of society?

One further point may be mentioned here. Just as in comparative doctrinal theology each theologian, working from within his own tradition, has to try to make sense of the other religions and their revelation-claims, so in the sphere of ethics, each moral theologian will need to make some sense of the high moral ideals and actual sainthood fostered in other faiths. The Christian moral theologian, for example, will see the infinite creator God, revealed in Jesus Christ, himself pure goodness and the source of all value in the world, not only as manifesting his self-sacrificial love in the person and fate of Christ, not only as inspiring the followers of Christ with something of that same love and making *them* the instruments of the establishment of his kingdom on earth, *but also* as the more or less hidden source of all comparable goodness elsewhere in the history of religions.

Secular ethics and religious ethics

But the external critic and the self-critical theologian alike will immediately point out that human goodness is not only a religious phenomenon. It is to be found in many places in individual and social human life outside the sphere of any religious commitment. Of course there is also much wickedness in the world, but that is true of the world of religion too. Indeed the moral theologian must reckon not only with non-religious goodness, but also with moral criticism of the history of religion from the secular moralist. Particularly since the time of the Enlightenment, the history of the Christian Church has been subjected to trenchant moral criticism by writers such as David Hume and Bertrand Russell. Church history has indeed contained many morally outrageous episodes, including the Inquisition, the wars of religion and the persecution of 'witches'. Moral criticism has also fixed on Christian belief in hell, Christian alleged disparagement of sexuality and so on. Similar criticisms are made of other religions. The allegedly tolerant Hindus participated in the inter-communal massacres that followed the independence of India and Pakistan. The quest for enlightenment and release often led to the neglect of the poor, whose fate in any case was believed to be the result of wickedness in previous lives. Such criticisms are commonplace in humanist writing and are indeed powerful criticisms.

Moral criticism of religious ethics goes deeper than this. It is held that a religious morality is incurably heteronomous – that is to say, morality is seen as a matter of following injunctions from above, delivered authoritatively and requiring obedience. Against this, secular moralists have stressed the autonomy of morals, the free responsibility of the moral agent in his decisions and acts. Religious morality has also been held to perpetuate an immature and childish dependence on a father-figure projected on to the sky. Another major criticism found in writers such as Russell is that a religious ethic tends to be a prudential ethic, commending goodness not for its own sake, but by promise of reward and threat of punishment.

The idea that morality is dependent on religion was criticised long ago by Plato in his dialogue, *Euthyphro*. Plato's criticism took the form of a dilemma. Is the pious or the good simply to be defined as what the gods love, or do the gods love something precisely because it is good? If the former is the case, then anything whatever, even torture, would be good, if the gods chose, arbitrarily, to approve it. If the latter is the case, then goodness is a reality independent of the gods. It exists already and is there waiting to be loved by them and anyone else. This dilemma is held to prove the independence of morality from religion.

A religious moralist might answer these criticisms along the following lines, taking them in reverse order:

1 The 'Euthyphro' dilemma

The dilemma is unreal, because both horns are unfairly put. The goodness which exists in human life is certainly there to be discerned independently of anything the gods may say. But that is only because it is part of God's creation anyway, and itself reflects the essential goodness of the divine creator. Nor is the good a matter of arbitrary definition by God. On the religious view, it is a fundamental fact that perfection belongs essentially to God's nature. Consequently it is out of the question that he might define something evil as good. In other words, there are two routes to knowledge of the good. We discern it in human nature and human relationships themselves, and we learn it (?less ambiguously) from revelation. The two sources – human nature and revelation-claims (for we never have revelation in a pure unmediated form) – are mutually corrective. Since both, ultimately, reflect the same essential divine perfection, they *cannot* ultimately conflict.

2 *The motives of reward and punishment*
These do not represent the highest insights of the religions. Christianity, for instance, is not, in essence, concerned to buttress its love ethic by threats and promises. It sets before us the self-sacrificial love of God in Christ as the ultimate inspiration and resource for ethical living. The *consequences* of such living or failure so to live may be spelled out by Jesus in the Sermon on the Mount, but they are not the *motive* for Christian response.

3 *The maturity of a religious morality*
There are two ways of dealing with this problem. One is to point to the lives of Christian saints and to the writings of the great moral theologians such as Dietrich Bonhoeffer and Reinhold Niebuhr, and ask whether in reasonable judgement these men can seriously be accused of immaturity. The other is to suggest that one cannot substantiate this criticism simply by assuming the truth of atheism. If in fact men find their own true good in relation to the infinite source of all being and value, then the manner in which they conform to the creature–creator relationship in which they exist may be immature or it may be mature. It depends on the stage of spiritual growth which they have reached.

4 *The autonomy of ethics*
On the one hand, the moral theologian will suggest that, if God is the one in whom we live and move and have our being, then the relation of dependence on ultimate

goodness just *is* the basic form of human flourishing. That dependence need not be a slavish one to an authoritarian father-figure. On the contrary, it may be the case that the infinitely good God deliberately refrains from imposing his will, but rather wins man's free response by the way of the cross. Such, at any rate, is the view of Christianity. On the other hand the moral theologian will point to ambiguities in the secular notion of a purely autonomous ethic. No one is denying that human goodness is found independently from religion. But that is a mysterious fact. There seems to be no rational basis for a *purely* autonomous ethic.

5 *The actual record of religion in history*

All the religions have cause for shame and repentance here. They cannot defend what has sometimes been done in their name. But moral theology can only plead for an evaluation of the ethical insights of the religions at their best and at their most profound.

Finally, a word may be added about the need for each religion's moral theologians to do justice to secular ethics and to natural human goodness, and to relate these phenomena to its own understanding of the ultimate source of all value. The way this is done will vary greatly between the religions. The theistic religions are in a position to urge, along the lines of our argument against the *Euthyphro* dilemma, that natural human goodness and the non-religious moral philosophies which investigate the notions of the right and the good as they function in human moral life are expressing and analysing what in reality are God-given facts about human interpersonal relations and human community. If man is made in the image of God, however far he may fall short of the ideal, his perception of human good cannot for long go flat against the actual structures that make for human flourishing. The theist will interpret these structures as God-given, and all actual human goodness as indicative of the Spirit of God in the world. The atheistic moralist will simply take them as they are as requiring no further grounding. Whether that is an ultimately rational position remains, as has been said, a question mark against a purely autonomous ethic.

One way of looking at morality in human life is to see it as operating on two levels. At one level, morality is a matter of fundamental interpersonal and social obligations. There can be agreement between the secular and the religious moralist at this level over what are the basic obligations – respect for life and property, for truth and justice and so on. The secular moralist may interpret these as the necessary conditions of human life in community. That is to give a utilitarian account of basic common morality, in other words, to defend these rules on grounds of their consequences for human well-being. The religious moralist may not disagree with this account, but he will want to go further and give an absolute status to respect for human life, and for truth and justice as ends in themselves, reflecting the nature and will of God. Nevertheless there can be agreement on this basic common morality. It is sometimes referred to as 'natural law'.

Over and above this basic common morality, however, there are much more demanding ideals of human life, including religious ones, which may be put forward for our acceptance. At this level there is widespread disagreement. As we have seen, the different religions may well stress different values and the secular moralist may reject aspects of them all. Contemplative values, ascetic values (extreme self-denial), spirituality, self-sacrifice may well not commend themselves to those who think of human good in terms of self-realisation. Again, the secular moralist may well see value in the very plurality of ideals of life which are put forward at this level, over and above the basic obligations. In other words he may deny that any high ideal of human life is of universal scope. The religious moralist will tend to disagree. The Christian, for example, can hardly suppose that the perfectionist love ethic of Jesus is just one option among others, to be chosen as a model by those who find it attractive. It is a characteristic of religious ideals to claim absoluteness and universal scope, just because they are held to reflect the nature and will of God himself. Hence the seriousness of the problem of conflicting religious ideals.

Individual and social ideals of human life

One of the main criticisms of religious ideals is that their stress on personal faith, on pure motives and individual commitment has led them to neglect the social dimension of human existence. Of course, the religions have never denied the social nature of morality altogether. Good will, compassion, forgiveness, love are interpersonal ideals and the relation between a man and his neighbour (including his enemy) has always been the focus of religious ethical concern. But quite apart from the problem of how central these concerns are in comparison with mystical and devotional ideals, the question still remains whether the religions have it in them to inspire and foster a just ordering of human society. Their concern for the neighbour and for the poor still seems to be a matter of shaping individual attitudes and inspiring individual acts of charity, rather than changing social structures. Even where the practical emphasis is to the fore, religion is thought of as a way of life, rather than an instrument of social change. Christianity, for example, which has always spoken of justice, and certainly contains a powerful religious impulse to help the poor, the sick and the unloved, has nevertheless, for much of its history, allied itself with the existing orders of society, and taught its members to respect the 'powers that be' and to see them as possessing a providential role in God's world. Christianity certainly has a social as well as an individual ideal, pictured in terms of the 'kingdom of God'. But this kingdom is held to be realisable on earth only through the preaching of the gospel, and through the allegiance and transformation of more and more individuals, who are then supposed to go on to manifest the qualities of Christian love.

The problem with this approach has been well brought out by Reinhold Niebuhr in his book, *Moral Man and Immoral Society.** He points out the moral confusion which results when the Christian Church encourages charity and benevolence in individuals within an unjust social system. The least well-placed in society are liable to experience such attitudes as hypocritical, when displayed by Christians with a relatively privileged position in society. The problem, Niebuhr argues, is greatly aggravated in an urbanised, industrial society. In a small-scale rural society, the unequal social relations were less sharply felt, since face-to-face personal relations were still a possibility for all involved. But this is much more difficult in the anonymity of city and industrial life. The underlying injustices are much more sharply exposed, and the benevolence of individuals much less acceptable as a substitute for social change, since it is bound either to be highly selective, or itself channelled through impersonal agencies.

The result of individual good will from within an unjust social system is moral cynicism on the part of the recipients. Much of the opposition to the Christian churches has stemmed from this cause.

On the other hand the attempt to change the structures of society in the interests of justice and equality, but without regard for individual morality, has led to even

---

* New York: Scribner's, 1932.

worse results. Marxist–Leninists have precipitated social revolution in many countries of the world, without regard for life, human rights, truth or love. The appalling consequences of such theoretically just political action, accompanied by unqualified moral cynicism, have been documented by writers such as Alexander Solzhenitsyn. The religions, with their stress on individual morality, have suffered badly in these situations, largely because of their inability to extract themselves from the previous unjust social systems. Yet the revival and persistence of religion in communist lands can be interpreted as a testimony to the basic moral and spiritual nature of man.

The question thus arises whether the religions have the resources to foster and sustain both an individual moral ideal *and* a practical social ideal of justice and equality. It has sometimes been felt that the answer is negative, and there is a strand in world religion which has seen it as necessary to withdraw from society in order to practise genuine charity. The classic example in the history of Christianity is that of St. Francis. The sense that only a man with no ties or stake in society at all can practise utterly disinterested love of the neighbour possesses great religious power. Part of the attraction of St Francis is his obvious lack of any kind of hypocrisy. Much the same considerations lie behind the attractiveness of the figure of Mother Theresa in the slums of Calcutta today. A religion which ceases to contain the power to inspire such unqualified dedication has undoubtedly lost something of its ethical and spiritual vision.

But Christianity has not remained content with the Franciscan ideal alone. In the light of the example of the Old Testament prophets, with their insistent demands for social justice, and in the light of the symbol of the kingdom of God, with its implication of God's will being done on earth, Christianity has never abandoned a definite social dimension in its ethical teaching. The Christian socialists in the nineteenth century, and church leaders

The problems of theology

such as William Temple in our own century, have kept the ideal of the social gospel alive, and it has recently become a dominant element in the deliberations and actions of the World Council of Churches. At an early stage in his career, Karl Barth went so far as to say that socialism is a predicate of the gospel, and, although he later saw reason to refrain from this unqualified assertion, since as a human political ideal socialism is as much subject to corruption and in need of criticism as any other human construct, he never ceased to try to spell out and urge the social implications of the Christian gospel.

Much stress has already been placed in the course of this book on the power of the great religions to develop and change creatively in face of new problems and changed conditions. It is probably true to say that the ethical ideals of Christianity and of other faiths too will in the future be found compelling only if they include a powerful social ethic as well as an individual vision of the good.

The relation between these two aspects of the religious ideal is itself an important and difficult problem. It can be raised crudely by asking which of the two has the priority. The answer seems to be that, at least for Christian moral theology, both are equally important. An individual ideal of life without commitment to social justice is as seriously distorted as a social concern without purity of heart. It is true that there are circumstances where it is impossible to *do* much about the structures of society. The early Christians exemplify this. They could transform society only indirectly by the example and attraction of transformed lives and by prophetic words. But in open societies, the individual and the Church can be judged to have failed in their Christian responsibilities if they cultivate private morality alone.

Of course Christianity does not postulate, as Marxism appears to do, the positive thrust of historical forces irrespective of what individuals think or do. In Christian

140

terms, the grace of God does not bypass the individual in bringing about the kingdom of God on earth. There may be negative constraints built into human interpersonal nature, whereby the will of God can never be permanently thwarted, but positively speaking, the providence of God is held to operate through the self-dedication of individual men and women to God's purposes. But those purposes are both individual and social. Christians are expected to work and pray equally for a Christ-like life and for the kingdom of God.

It is clear that Christians do not have a monopoly of social ethical concern. Considerations advanced earlier in this chapter on the phenomenon of non-Christian, including secular, goodness must be expanded here to include the widespread evidence of social concern outside the borders of any or all religion. Consequently Christian social ethics would have to include a readiness to co-operate with all men of good will in working for a just and humane world. That is to say, from the Christian point of view, that while the providence of God does not bypass the individual heart and mind, it does not restrict itself to the self-consciously Christian heart and mind.

8

The problem of doctrine today

Is doctrine important?

Anthropologists have concentrated attention on religious rites and the role which they play in the lives of different peoples. Sociologists have concentrated attention on religious institutions and their function in society. Much has been said about the way in which religious symbols and myths bring to expression deeprooted psychological and cultural constants in human life. As we saw in the last chapter, it is possible to concentrate on the ethical dimension of religion to the neglect or exclusion of others, so that religion is seen simply as a means of reinforcing an all-embracing moral ideal. All these approaches encourage us to play down the place of doctrines and beliefs in religion. But closer phenomenological attention to the history of religions shows that explicitly or implicitly the rituals, institutions and practices of the religions are shaped and conditioned by beliefs, which can be made the object of critical reflection, if not always by the participant, then by the student of religion.

Clearly these beliefs are often very primitive, and intelligible only in relation to the pre-scientific world-view of non-literate tribes or early civilisations. Even the theologian can hardly take them at their face value, but will interpret them as highly inadequate means of expressing some sense of the holy or of the divine. But in the course of time, and usually under the influence of major creative religious personalities, the so-called 'higher' religions have developed systematic and all-embracing doctrinal schemes, spelling out what they see as the fundamental truths about the world and man. The theistic religions have done so under the conviction that the world and man can be understood rightly only in relation to God, though they have differed in the conception of his nature and his purpose.

It is important to realise that the major world religions have usually felt quite free to call upon the resources of philosophy as an aid in the articulation of a comprehensive and metaphysically plausible world-view. We saw in Chapter 4 something of this interplay between theology and philosophy. Moreover, since the rise of modern science, the religions have had to rethink the whole God–world relation, both in respect of our knowledge of the causal factors operating in the created world, and in respect of a purer concept of the transcendent and immanent God. The success with which they do this is a measure of their capacity to grow and flourish in the future.

Religious belief, then, about God, man and the universe is an increasingly important dimension in the history of religions. It cannot be claimed that the average believer in any religion has a full command of the whole world-view, with all its interconnecting doctrines, that has been developed and articulated over the centuries. There is a sense in which he inherits a given tradition, which is constantly being worked over and interpreted afresh by each generation of the religion's theologians and teachers. But he appropriates this tradition for himself to a greater or lesser degree through instruction, liturgy and practical participation in the religious life of the community. With the increase of education each participant will wish to share more himself in the reflective approach to his tradition's world-view which we call 'theology'.

The importance of doctrine lies precisely in the fact that religion is more than a set of attitudes and rites. It contains a marked cognitive element, purporting to yield knowledge of the way things ultimately are. Only if the truth about God, man and the universe can be discovered, can the will of God be done knowingly and human life lived in some conscious and justified expectancy of its ultimate destiny. Equally the sympathetic though uncommitted observer of religion will want to know precisely what it is that is being put forward for belief.

The difference between doctrines and myths

The question at once arises whether it is possible to convey ultimate truths directly. It is widely believed that religious truth can be communicated only indirectly through myths and parables and a variety of symbolic forms of language and action. There is much in the history of religion to support this view. The Buddha's rejection of metaphysical speculation about ultimate realities is well known. So is the fact that Jesus taught by parable and conveyed more by the manner of his life and death than by straight teaching. Some philosophers have asserted that all religious doctrines and metaphysical systems are themselves on a par with myths and symbols, pointing blindly to an unknowable transcendence. The Swiss philosopher, Karl Jaspers (1883–1969), calls them 'ciphers', holding that they reflect an encounter with the transcendent which, in the nature of the case, cannot be put into cognitive propositional form. Some theologians, too, have taught the symbolic nature of all religious language. With the dubious exception of the assertion that God is 'Being Itself', Paul Tillich held that all talk about God is symbolic. By a symbol, in the religious case, he meant a 'segment of finite reality' which comes to be seen or felt to point beyond itself to an infinite reality in which it somehow participates. If it ceases to be felt that way, the symbol has gone dead on people.*

If we are to distinguish the doctrinal dimension from the mythical dimension in religion, we shall have to resist this conflation of myth, symbol, parable and doctrine. Without denying that religious truth is often conveyed most graphically by myths and parables, we should have to show that it is possible to state, more prosaically in non-parabolic form, at least something of what was being conveyed pictorially or dramatically in the myths and parables. It can be argued that this was what the early Fathers of the Christian Church were doing as they hammered out the doctrines of the Trinity and incarnation, though the process goes right back to the New Testament writers too.

A few remarks on 'myth', 'symbol' and 'parable' are called for at this point, in order to bring out the contrast with 'doctrine'.

'Myth' is an extremely elusive term in the context of religion. In popular usage, it seems to mean little more than 'falsehood', and tends to carry a derogatory sense. We say that some story is *only* a myth or fairy tale. There are many such myths in the folk-lore of religion. There is no *need* to condemn them. We do not condemn the myths of Greece and Rome, though they are certainly not true in any literal sense. The possibility remains that such fictitious stories may convey some deeper truth, say, about the seasons or the dependence of man on the natural processes of rain and sun. In early religion, such dependence may be given religious overtones and thus itself symbolise man's dependence on divine power.† Thus there may be an even deeper truth underlying the surface story or myth. Jung held that many of the common features in religious myths express indirectly

* P. Tillich, *Systematic Theology*, vol. I (London: Nisbet, 1953), pp. 265ff.
† On symbol, see p. 147, below.

some very fundamental truths about man (though he did not commit himself on whether they also expressed fundamental truths about God).* In developed religion, it is clear that myths can be used to express much more obviously certain fundamental religious beliefs. Thus the creation myths in Genesis 1 and 2, though not literally true, express very vividly the belief that all things depend for their being in being on the creative acts of God. That belief can be expressed straightforwardly in doctrine – viz the doctrine of creation. The concept of 'creation' is not itself mythological. It uses an analogy from human creative action, qualifies it by excluding finite elements, and asserts it categorically of the infinite. It is this possibility of analogical prediction that differentiates doctrine from myth.† The underlying doctrine which the myth expresses pictorially and in story form, can be extracted and expressed propositionally by means of analogy.

It is always an important question: What precisely is the doctrine that underlies a religious myth? In the case of the Judaeo-Christian creation myths, the answer is quite clear: it is the doctrine of the world's dependence on infinite mind or spirit for its being in being at all. In recent Christian theology the question has been raised whether the incarnation is a myth or a doctrine. Some theologians have suggested that the story of the descent of the Son of God from heaven to live a human life and die a human death and then to rise again to the right hand of the Father is purely mythological. There are undoubtedly some pictorial, mythological elements in this story. But the important question is, Precisely what underlying truth is being expressed here? What is the doctrine behind the myth? Is it the claim that in essence

* See pp. 48f., above.
† On analogy, see p. 71, above.

and ideal God and man are one? In other words, Does it express the general unity or identity of the human and the divine, as Hegel apparently thought? Or does it rather express the belief that God himself, without ceasing to be God, has come amongst us out of love for mankind, and revealed himself in a human life and death? Phenomenological faithfulness to the Christian tradition will lead the student of Christian theology to accept the latter answer, and insist on speaking not of the myth, but of the *doctrine* of the incarnation.

'Symbol' is also a difficult concept to analyse. One thing can stand for another in ordinary life, either by convention or by some natural connection or both. Thus the symbols on the television weather forecast charts resemble, pictorially, the clouds or rain which they symbolise. In human social life, the nation's flag may come to symbolise the nation's presence and power, simply by association and conventional use. In poetry, the fire and the rose may become powerful symbols, as they do in T. S. Eliot's *Four Quartets*, of the supernatural and the natural. In religion, too, concepts or images, such as 'king' and 'father' may come, in the course of the tradition, to function as symbols of the divine, of God's sovereign power and rule, and of his universal care and providence. Such symbols have a long history of religious use, and it is possible to trace the ways in which they have been qualified and profoundly transformed, often quite paradoxically, as in the Christian picture of the one who rules from the cross. But again, as with the case of myth, the realities which the symbols symbolise can at least in part be expressed and formulated in terms of doctrine, using non-symbolic though still analogical language.

'Parable' is an easier concept to handle. It is a form of oral or written teaching, which deliberately sets out some moral or religious truth in the form of an anecdote which

147

strikes home to the heart. There is no question here of the parabolic form obscuring the moral or doctrinal content. Rather it conveys it vividly (except to the hard-hearted).

Doctrine, then, attempts to set out propositionally the truth-content that lies behind or is embedded in the myths, symbols and parables of religion. No doubt it loses something of the religious force of those more vivid forms, and the limitations of analogical discourse no doubt render its attempts to state the truth about God and the world partial and at best approximate. But only if the truths conveyed by myth, symbol and parable are spelled out in terms of doctrine, can their interconnections and their comprehensive nature be shown.

For it is clear that, in the study of doctrine, one is not dealing with particular isolated beliefs, which can be scrutinised apart from all the other elements in a given religion. Doctrine is essentially systematic, not in the sense of a fixed and static body of interconnected axioms and deductions, but in the sense of yielding a comprehensive view of all men's discoveries and all men's experience. To understand Christian doctrine, for example, we have to appreciate the interrelation of all its elements, the way its concept of God is determined by its understanding of Jesus Christ, and the way its doctrine of man is determined by its understanding of creation, history and the future, which themselves depend on the fundamental theology and Christology. Moreover, as we stressed in Chapter 1, theology is not an omniscient science. For all its drive towards comprehensive vision, it has to reckon with its human limitations, and recognise the points at which it *can* speak only of mystery and transcendence, and admit that God remains hidden even in his revelation. Moreover Christian doctrine is essentially concerned with an active God, whose reality may be expected to impinge on man in unpredictable ways. The comprehensive world-view which Christian doctrine seeks to articulate has to leave room for openness to a living and present spiritual relation between God and man.

The possibility of doctrinal theology

Is such a doctrinal theology possible? We have seen in the course of this book that there are very grave problems about the whole enterprise. Unlike the case of natural science, there is in the world of religion a mass of conflicting data, and no agreed method whereby the truth can be established to the satisfaction of all. Admittedly the case of natural science is not so fixed as this formulation suggests, and it too is subject to startling transformations and revisions. Its results are thus inescapably provisional. But the criteria of the growth of scientific knowledge are agreed. In religion, by contrast, we have a number of different historical traditions usually claiming special revelation as their source, and interpreting the world and human life in very different ways. We have examined some of the problems which arise when we become aware of the socially, culturally and historically conditioned nature of the developing systems of belief in each major religion.

Nevertheless we are talking about living traditions in which people today stand in continuity with their predecessors in the faith down the ages. We can at least make the experiment of examining a given tradition as a possible key for the interpretation of the universe. We can look at its origins so far as they are known. We can see how each generation within the tradition has expressed its understanding of its own faith and the light which it has thrown on the nature and meaning of the world and human life. We can follow the way in which that tradition's theologians, employing every philosophical resource at their command, have articulated the common faith systematically, and related it to historical and scientific knowledge. In the modern age of critical thinking, we can try to judge how well the foundation documents and what has developed out of them in terms of doctrinal synthesis have been able to stand up to critical probing and investigation. We can try to see how well the tradition's faith works out in practice in terms of spiritual growth and ethical profundity.

But we cannot remain uncritically within the horizon of a single tradition. We have also, as has been urged throughout this book, to see how well a given tradition can make sense of all the other religions in the world, and we have to enter into dialogue with theologians in other traditions who are conducting similar investigations from their different starting points. As we attempt to familiarise ourselves with their religious systems and their views of other faiths, we would hope to be able to reach some assessment both of the common ground and of the differences. Above all, we have to ask ourselves whether the unique and allegedly normative elements in any one particular tradition can really maintain their universality in a pluralistic religious world. Only such rigorously pursued comparative theology can overcome the problem of the absence of a single starting point in the epistemology of religion.

We conclude this book by giving two illustrations of this enterprise, using as examples the cases of Hinduism and Christianity.

Hindu doctrines of God and incarnation

Hinduism would seem to be well placed in the enterprise of comparative theology. This ancient religion is itself very varied in form and doctrine. It rests less on particular revelation than on a long tradition of spiritual wisdom and devotional enthusiasm. It is not dependent on a particular series of historical events. It is capable, at least to some extent, of accommodating to itself the results of modern science, as, for example, in the evolutionary theology of Sri Aurobindo (1872–1950).

The problem of doctrine today

Above all, it readily includes the recognition of other religions as paths to the same goal. All this means, of course, that doctrine in Hinduism is very varied and flexible, and that much more is conceded to the realm of myth than in historical Christianity. The point of the religion seems more to foster a deep spirituality, whether of a mystical or of a devotional kind.

Of course, there are doctrines in Hinduism. There is a characteristic view of the world as cyclical rather than historical (despite the evolutionary views of Aurobindo), and of human life as repetitive, caught in the wheel of rebirth, till mystical or devotional release is achieved. There are characteristic doctrines of God. It has already been pointed out that the form of Hinduism most familiar in the west, the more philosophical Advaita Vedānta, is not the most characteristic form, since its treatment of divine personality as a lower-level accommodation to the devotee, and its preference for a higher-level impersonal absolute, beyond all human description, are very different from the devotional religion of the Indian villages, and indeed from the most popular Hindu scripture, the Bhagavad Gītā. It is more characteristic to see the many gods of popular Hinduism as different facets or foci of the one God, Vishnu, or, in another strand of Hindu devotional religion, Shiva. The ultimate here remains personal, as in the theology of Rāmānuja, who interprets philosophical Vedānta in the light of devotional Vaishnavite* religion, rather than vice versa.†

The most striking of the Vaishnavite doctrines is that of the Avatārs, incarnations of Vishnu, who descends to earth in times of special need, to bring help and inspiration to men. The best known of these is Krishna, whose advice and revelations are found in the Bhagavad Gītā.

* Vaishnavites are worshippers of Vishnu.
† On Rāmānuja, see p. 68, above.

But it is important to recall that there are many Avatārs in Vaishnavite belief, some in animal form. The flexibility of this doctrine is very great. It is possible for Vaishnavites to see the great figures of other faiths, such as the Buddha or Jesus, as incarnations of the divine, and the principle is often extended to Gandhi and any striking spiritual leader in the present day. Indeed, according to Radhakrishnan, all conscious beings are potentially divine, and Avatārs are special manifestations of the universal divine spirit in order to help us become what we potentially are.

It will readily be seen how easily Hinduism can develop a theology of religion and the religions such as we have envisaged as a necessity for any religion in a pluralistic religious world. The cost of such flexibility, it might be argued, is vagueness. The problem for Hinduism, so the critic would say, remains that of identifying who God is. For all the wisdom, spirituality and devotion fostered in the Hindu tradition, it remains a question mark against Hindu theology, whether its chameleon-like quality of embracing every religious faith as a path to the same goal, does not evacuate its faith of recognisable content. In Hindu–Christian dialogue, the Christian is bound to ask what it means for faith in God, that such different individuals (including animals) can manifest God to man, that the supreme God is himself so differently represented in the Vaishnavite and Shaivite strands, and that a powerful philosophical movement (Advaita Vedānta) reduces all personal faith to a provisional stage in the journey towards identification with the Absolute Brahman, beyond all attributes.

Christian doctrines of the incarnation and Trinity

Christianity, with its emphasis on a particular historical revelation, and the consequent normativeness of Jesus Christ for human knowledge of God and eventual union with God, would seem to be much less well placed to develop a theology of religion and the religions that does justice to the spirituality and religious power of other faiths. It is not surprising that some Christian theologians are themselves attempting to play down the uniqueness and absoluteness of Christ, in the interests of seeing Christian faith in God as just one among many religiously creative, yet partial and relative, approaches to the knowledge and love of God.

In order to judge the rights and wrongs of this internal Christian dispute, as well as to judge the ability of a more traditional Christianity both to make out its own case and to account for spirituality elsewhere, the student will need to investigate fairly the content and scope of Christian doctrine.

Traditionally, what has distinguished Christian faith from other monotheistic world religions has been its doctrines of the incarnation and the Trinity. It is perfectly true that many Christians have simply been inspired by the figure of Jesus in the gospels and wished in some sense to associate themselves with the Christian Church as disciples and believers, without subscribing to or even understanding the doctrines of the incarnation and the Trinity, enshrined in the Christian creeds. Nevertheless the theologian will not be willing to investigate Christianity only in its minimal forms; he will be bound to try to think systematically and at least explore the fundamental doctrines which the councils, creeds and confessions down the ages have seen as expressing the essence of Christianity. There are of course many differences between the various formulations, the fundamental doctrines have been very variously understood within the Christian Church, and there is no reason to suppose that Christian doctrine is a fixed and static affair, incapable of development and reformulation. On the contrary, if there is a common thread running through the discussion of the problems of theology in this book, it is the necessity of reckoning with both continuity and change in the transmission of traditions through very different social and cultural milieux. But it can hardly be denied that throughout nearly two thousand years of Christian history, the doctrines of the incarnation and Trinity have summed up the special features of Christian belief as to who God is.

What is it that those doctrines state? They state the belief that the infinite and eternal God, who brought the world into being and sustains its whole evolving history, made himself known to his human creatures as being essentially self-sacrificial love, by coming into our midst himself, and winning the response of human recognition and love, freely given in gratitude and dedication. The conditions of such an incarnation were, on the human side, the emergence of a particular historical context, a tradition of faith in terms of which the life of Jesus could be construed as God's own human life, and, on the divine side, a God whose very being included different modes of being, related one to the other in the relation of love. For the relation of Jesus to his heavenly Father was recognised to mirror and reveal the inner love within the Godhead. This was the starting point of the doctrine of the Trinity, the necessity of thinking of God in relational terms being a consequence of belief in the divinity of Christ. At the same time it was clear that incarnation did not mean the total transformation of God into man. That would be an absurd idea. On the contrary it was recognised that God's infinite and eternal reality must be such as to include the possibility of becoming man without ceasing to be God in any way. Equally humanity was not so alien to the creator as to be incapable of being united to one of the modes of God's own being in an incarnate life. The further doctrine of the Spirit was a consequence of the sense that God's presence in the heart of the believer was a different mode of 'being present' from that of the incarnation. Indeed it could equally well be spoken of as the presence in the believer of the Spirit of the risen Christ.

All this doctrine was not spun out of men's imaginations. It represented the intellectual and rational response of men on whom the life and death and resurrection of Jesus had made an unparalleled and overwhelming impression. If this man was indeed the Son of God in person ('The Son' became a symbolic phrase for that mode of God's being which was made man), then there was a sense in which people could know God personally, over and above the intimations and experiences of the holy, which they could already enjoy. Moreover it is not difficult to see that real *personal* knowledge requires a single incarnation. A series of human beings could manifest only certain *general* qualities in God, whereas, for Christians, Jesus Christ, risen and ascended, is for ever the human, personal focus of our knowledge of God. There was also a deep moral sense in which God had made himself credible by accepting responsibility for all the world's ills, by submitting himself to suffering, despair and death. This could not be done by a representative, someone other than himself.

So it came about that Christianity grew upon the conviction that the trinitarian God of love had made himself personally knowable and known by coming amongst us as a man. This conviction led to many further consequences – for example, the conviction that human history must be regarded as a single process, leading first to the incarnation, and from that point to the eventual all-inclusive gathering up of humanity into the God whom Christ makes known.

As Christians have confronted the non-Christian world, their response has been both practical and theoretical. They have gone out to evangelise and to serve, to share the knowledge of God in Christ, and to follow his example. Theologically, they have learned to look for the presence of Christ already in hidden and implicit ways in

other faiths and in human love, wherever it is found.
They have lived in the confidence that, in God's eternity,
these other ways will be taken up and transfigured into
explicit recognition of the trinitarian God whom Christ
reveals.

These doctrines will be scrutinised by the theologian
for their ability to make sense of the whole world of religion and life. They will be compared with other theologies, such as the Hindu theology of many different
Avatārs, each manifesting the divine, wherever he
occurs, and evaluated according to the criteria set out in
Chapter 2 (pp. 38–43). Such comparative work is only
beginning to be done, and it is still marred by failure to
overcome the sheer difficulty of doing justice, in such
comparisons, to the views of one's colleagues in other
faiths. Comparison is made even more difficult by the
current tendency in Christian theology to reduce the
characteristic Christian doctrines to something that
could be said by Hindus anyway. Such agreement is too
cheaply gained.

Conclusion

Doctrine, then, is not to be despised. It is to be studied by
theologians in every tradition in its full depth and systematic range. Fully alive to the historical relativity and
cultural conditionedness of any one religion's understanding of the world, the theologian will nevertheless
recognise the continuities and all-embracing scope of the
great world faiths. As he studies the history of religions,
he will certainly be on the look-out for common ground,
both in doctrine and ethics, but he will not rule out *a
priori* the possibility that in the midst of the vagaries and
relativities of history, there has been given a definitive
revelation of who God is and what is to be done. Any
such purported revelation will of course be expressed in
all too human words, and the varied developing formula-

tions must be criticised and tested both for their inner rationality and for their power to illuminate the whole of reality. Dialogue between believers of different faiths will involve comparison not only of the religious systems themselves, but of what they make of each other and of the whole religious life of man. The unbeliever will wish to put his questions to them all, as they theirs to him.

Doctrinal theology in all its aspects is undertaken in the hope that from the interplay and mutual testing of the different proposals for belief that have been made throughout the history of religions, the truth will be found to have emerged. In the meantime, the theologian, like any other man, will try to live by the truth that he has so far seen.

Select bibliography

The nature and scope of theology

Introductory works

Healey, F. G. (ed.), *Preface to Christian Studies*, London: Lutterworth, 1971

Hordern, W., *Introduction to Theology*, London: Lutterworth, 1968

Sykes, S. W., *Christian Theology Today*, London: Mowbrays, 1971

Wiles, M., *What is Theology?*, London: OUP, 1976

Advanced works

Lonergan, B., *Method in Theology*, London: Darton, Longman and Todd, 1972

Pannenberg, W., *Theology and the Philosophy of Science*, English trans., London: Darton, Longman and Todd, 1976

Comparative religion

Introductory works

Bouquet, A. C., *Comparative Religion*, Harmondsworth: Penguin Books, 1941

Holm, J., *The Study of Religions*, London: Sheldon Press, 1977

Sharpe, E. J., *Comparative Religion: a History*, London: Duckworth, 1975

Smart, N., *The Phenomenon of Religion*, London: Macmillan, 1973

Advanced works

Christian, W. A., *Meaning and Truth in Religion*, Princeton University Press, 1964

Select bibliography

van der Leeuw, G., *Religion in Essence and Manifestation*, English trans., London: Allen and Unwin, 1938, and New York: Harper and Row (Harper Torchbooks edition), 1963

The scientific study of religion

Introductory works

Berger, P. L., *The Social Reality of Religion*, London: Faber and Faber, 1969, and Harmondsworth: Penguin Books, 1973

Evans-Pritchard, E. E., *Theories of Primitive Religion*, Oxford: Clarendon Press, 1965

Gill, R., *Social Context of Theology*, London: Mowbrays, 1975

Smart, N., *The Science of Religion and the Sociology of Knowledge*, Princeton University Press, 1973

Advanced works

Bowker, J., *The Sense of God*, Oxford: Clarendon Press, 1973

Yinger, J. M., *The Scientific Study of Religion*, New York: Macmillan, 1970

Philosophy of religion

Introductory works

Baelz, P. R., *Christian Theology and Metaphysics*, London: Epworth Press, 1968

Hick, J., *Philosophy of Religion*, second edition, Englewood Cliffs, N. J.: Prentice-Hall, 1973

Lewis, H. D., *Philosophy of Religion* (Teach Yourself Books), London: The English Universities Press, 1965

Advanced works

Farrer, A. M., *Faith and Speculation*, London: A. & C. Black, 1967

Mitchell, B., *The Justification of Religious Belief*, London: Macmillan, 1973

Newman, J. H., *A Grammar of Assent*, London: Burns, Oates, 1870

Select bibliography

Revelation

Introductory works

Baillie, J., *The Idea of Revelation in Recent Thought*, London: OUP, 1956
Farmer, H. H., *Revelation and Religion*, London: Nisbet, 1954
Stacey, D., *Interpreting the Bible*, London: Sheldon Press, 1976

Advanced works

Murty, K. S., *Revelation and Reason in Advaita Vedānta*, London: OUP, 1956
Pannenberg, W. (ed.), *Revelation as History*, English trans., London: Sheed and Ward, 1969

History and theology

Introductory works

Barr, J., *The Bible in the Modern World*, London: SCM Press, 1973
Niebuhr, R., *Faith and History*, London: Nisbet, 1949
Richardson, A., *Science, History and Faith*, London: OUP, 1950

Advanced works

Harvey, V. A., *The Historian and the Believer*, London: SCM Press, 1967
Morgan, R., and Pye, M. (eds.), *Ernst Troeltsch: Writings on Theology and Religion*, London: Duckworth, 1977

Ethics

Introductory works

Baelz, P. R., *Ethics and Belief*, London: Sheldon Press, 1977
Danto, A. C., *Mysticism and Morality*, New York: Basic Books Inc., 1972, and Harmondsworth: Penguin Books, 1976
Niebuhr, R., *Moral Man and Immoral Society*, New York: Scribner's 1932
Radhakrishnan, S., *The Hindu View of Life*, London: Allen and Unwin, 1927

Select bibliography

Advanced works

Bonhoeffer, D., *Ethics*, London: SCM Press, 1955
Kirk, K. E., *The Vision of God*, London: Longmans, 1931

Doctrine

Introductory works

Farrer, A. M., *Saving Belief*, London: Hodder and Stoughton, 1964
Pannenberg, W., *Faith and Reality*, English trans., London: Search Press, and Philadelphia: Westminster Press, 1977
Parrinder, G., *Avatar and Incarnation*, London: Faber and Faber, 1970
Smart, N., *The Yogi and the Devotee*, London: Allen and Unwin, 1968
Wiles, M., *The Remaking of Christian Doctrine*, London: SCM Press, 1974

Advanced work

Cunliffe-Jones, H. (ed.), *A History of Christian Doctrine*, Edinburgh: T. & T. Clark, 1979

Index

Index